The
POWER
⤠ of ⤟
APPRECIATION

The Key to a Vibrant Life

The
POWER
of
APPRECIATION

The Key to a Vibrant Life

NOELLE C. NELSON, Ph.D. and
JEANNINE LEMARE CALABA, Psy.D.

BEYOND
WORDS
Publishing
I N C

Beyond Words Publishing, Inc.
20827 N.W. Cornell Road, Suite 500
Hillsboro, Oregon 97124-9808
503-531-8700

Note: Names and other identifying details of Appreciators Group members have been changed to protect their privacy.

Editor: Laura Foster
Managing editor: Julie Steigerwaldt
Copyeditor: David Abel
Cover image: © George Lepp/ Getty Images
Cover design: Alexandra Graham
Interior design: Dorral Lukas
Illustration: Darryl Anka
Composition: William H. Brunson Typography Services

Printed in the United States of America
Distributed to the book trade by Publishers Group West

Library of Congress Cataloging-in-Publication Data
Nelson, Noelle C.
    The power of appreciation : the key to a vibrant life / Noelle C. Nelson, Jeannine Lemare Calaba.
        p. cm.
Includes bibliographical references.
    ISBN 1-58270-104-0
    1. Gratitude.   2. Values—Psychological aspects.   I. Calaba, Jeannine Lemare.   II. Title.

BF575.G68N45   2003
179'.9—dc22
                                                                    2003015294

The corporate mission of Beyond Words Publishing, Inc.:
Inspire to Integrity

CONTENTS

Contents

ACKNOWLEDGMENTS

There is so much to appreciate in the making of this book. We are, of course, infinitely grateful to the members of our Appreciators Groups, for daring to explore with us a road truly less traveled. Our unbounded appreciation goes to Jerry and Esther Hicks, whose Abraham works have been a profound source of inspiration to us both as individuals and as authors. We extend our heartfelt thanks to Cynthia Black and Richard Cohn of Beyond Words, for seeing the potential in our original manuscript and helping us develop it, and to our editor, Laura Foster, for her unerring skill and patience. Special thanks go to Diane Rumbaugh, for her unending enthusiasm, good humor, hard work, and invaluable ideas, and to Michelle Masamitsu, for her amazing willingness to help out wherever needed.

For permission to quote from copyrighted materials, we are grateful to the following: from *The Grateful Disposition: A Conceptual and Empirical Topography* by M. McCullough, R. Emmons, & J. Tsang, *Journal of Personality and Social Psychology*, 82 (1), 2002, pp. 112–127. Copyright © 2002 by the American Psychological Association. Reprinted (or Adapted) with permission; from Dr. Edward Shafranske, Professor of Clinical Psychology, Pepperdine University, for his interview with Dr. Calaba, 1988; from *Ageless Body, Timeless Mind* by Deepak Chopra, copyright © 1993 by Deepak Chopra. Used by permission of Harmony Books, a division of Random House, Inc.; from *Waking the Tiger: Healing Trauma* by Peter A. Levine with Ann Frederick, North Atlantic Books, Berkeley, CA. Copyright © 1997 Peter A. Levine. Used by permission of the publisher; submitted excerpt from *The HeartMath Solution* by Doc Childre and Howard Martin. Copyright © 1999 by

The Institute of HeartMath. Reprinted by permission of HarperCollins Publishers Inc.; reprinted with permission from *Raising a Son* by Don Elium & Jeannie Elium. Copyright © 1996 by Jeannie Elium & Don Elium, Celestial Arts, Berkeley, CA. Available from your local bookseller, by calling Ten Speed Press at 800-841-2665, or by visiting us online at www.tenspeed.com; from *Research Suggests Positive Attitude Could Prolong Life* by Steve Bailey. Copyright © 2001 by The Associated Press. Reprinted with permission of The Associated Press; excerpts from *NO CONTEST: The Case Against Competition* by Alfie Kohn. Copyright © 1986 by Alfie Kohn. Reprinted by permission of Houghton Mifflin Company. All rights reserved; from *Aboard Flight 564* by Peter Hannaford. Copyright © 2001 News World Communications, Inc. Reprinted with permission of The Washington Times; from *Mindfulness* by Ellen Langer. Copyright © 1990 by Perseus Books Group, New York; from *Winner Takes All* by Noelle Nelson. Copyright © 1999 by Perseus Books Group, New York; from *Learning to Walk Again* from *Experts* by David Zucchino. Copyright © 2003, Los Angeles Times. Reprinted with permission; from Dr. Daniel Amen, Amen Behavioral Clinic, Newport Beach, California, for his SPECT scan analysis, 2002; from *Messages from Water* by Dr. Masaru Emoto. Copyright © 2000 by HADO Kyoikusha, Tokyo, Japan; from *Affect Regulation and the Origin of the Self* by Allan Schore. Copyright © 1994 by Lawrence Erlbaum Associates, New Jersey; from *Effects of a secure attachment relationship on right brain development, affect regulation, and infant mental health* by Allan Schore. Copyright © 2001 by Infant Mental Health Journal 22(1–2), pp. 7–66; from *The Art of Happiness* by HH Dalai Lama & Howard C. Cutler with translator, Dr. Thupten Jinpa. Copyright © 1998 by Riverhead Books, on imprint of Penguin Group (USA) Inc.; Reprinted with the permission of Scribner, an imprint of Simon & Schuster Adult Publishing Group, from *Molecules of Emotion* by Candace B. Pert. Copyright © 1997 by Candace B. Pert.

PREFACE

A few years back, a book title popped into my mind: *Count Your Blessings*. I thought, "That's nice," and wrote it on a post-it note (along with a list of other potential titles that had occurred to me over the years), and pretty much forgot about it.

A year or so later, I heard through a mutual friend that a fellow psychologist, Dr. Jeannine Lemare Calaba, was working with brain wave biofeedback. In my therapy practice, I had been using meditation and guided visualizations with considerable success as a way of helping people make profound changes in their lives. I was curious to see if the level of consciousness at which people make the shifts in awareness and understanding that lead to life changes would in some way be reflected in brain wave activity.

So I called Jeannine up, introduced myself, and asked if I could explore brain wave activity with her. She agreed, and for a couple of months we had a lot of fun working with my brain waves and getting to know one another. And yes, we did find that there appeared to be distinct changes in brain wave activity during meditation and other "altered states"; and no, I didn't particularly want to launch into a whole new area of research. End of story—or so I thought.

In my work both as a trial consultant and as a psychotherapist, I had become increasingly aware that people with a basically optimistic, positive, and appreciative approach to life had higher overall levels of satisfaction and fulfillment than those who adopted a more negative and disgruntled attitude toward things. From the research that I did for my book *Winner Takes All: Exceptional People*

Teach Us How to Find Career and Personal Success in the 21st Century, I had
realized that winners from all walks of life distinguished themselves by their phenomenal ability to appreciate in situations where others would despair.

I became even more intrigued by the role appreciation could play in our success and happiness when I realized (through my research on the prevention of
domestic violence for my book *Dangerous Relationships*) that, unlike abusive
individuals, nonabusive individuals are "appreciators"—that is to say, they value
and are grateful for themselves, other people, and life itself.

Fast-forward a couple of years. By this point, I've started deliberately working with appreciation in my practice as a way of helping people change both
their inner circumstances (how they think and feel) and their outer circumstances
(their relationships with people and the world around them), and I'm getting
excellent results.

One day, I'm staring at my list of post-its, just musing, and I think, "I wonder if your brain shows very different activity when you're counting your blessings, when you're appreciating." I had a hunch that if it did, it would probably
look much like brain waves do when we meditate.

So I call Jeannine and ask, "Can we take a look at my brain wave activity
when I'm appreciating?"

Jeannine (being the good sport that she is) says, "Sure." She hooks me up
with electrodes to the EEG software on her computer, takes a baseline measure-
ment, and then asks me to go into an appreciative state.

I'm appreciating with all my heart and mind, while Jeannine is observing the
computer screen and taking notes.

After what seems like forever, Jeannine says, "Well, your brain waves are
changing. Your focus is increasing and it looks like your brain waves are synchronizing."

"Synchronizing how? Doing what?" I ask excitedly.

"I don't have sophisticated enough equipment to say anything definite," Jeannine replies cautiously, "but some kind of pattern seems to be emerging."

Now I'm really intrigued. We don't know what's going on, but we have a strong feeling that we are on to something. If appreciation alters brain wave activity, then (given the well-known connection between mind and body) we expect that appreciation could have a beneficial effect on the body—just as stress, anger, and resentment have a negative effect. In addition, since brain waves can be a reflection of emotional states, appreciation may also have a positive impact on how you perceive the world around you and your relationship to it, as well as on how you feel.

We start to read everything we can find regarding scientific discoveries about the impact of appreciation on the body. To our delight, we find that many researchers have measured physiological activity (particularly heart rate variability and brain wave activity) under various emotional conditions, and found that in a state of appreciation, good things happen to your mind, heart, and body: your heart rate slows, your blood pressure drops, and your digestion is facilitated. You feel more peaceful, your stress diminishes, and your immune system benefits.

What we rarely find, however, is research that takes the crucial next step—using appreciation proactively to change life circumstances—or that answers questions such as:

- How can we use appreciation to improve health, relationships, and work life?
- How can the conscious use of appreciation increase success and happiness?
- How should we use appreciation to transform challenging situations, to effect changes in our lives, and to resolve crises?

Over the next three years, as Jeannine and I explore ways to use appreciation deliberately and purposefully to effect change in our own and in our patients' lives, we discover its true vibrational nature—that is, we discover that appreciation is an energy, a source of power you can use to transform those aspects of your life that aren't giving you the happiness and fulfillment you seek, and to make what does work in your life even better.

We develop techniques and tools, based on appreciation's vibrational quality. We test these techniques and tools with the cooperation and help of our clients, our friends, and the wonderful members of Appreciators Groups (AGs). We created these support groups as a forum for people to share their thoughts and ideas about appreciation; to learn how to use appreciation proactively and purposefully; and to inform, empower, brainstorm, troubleshoot, and support each other as they learn to use the energy of appreciation in their lives.

Along the way, we find not only that appreciation does work, but that it works in surprising and unexpected ways. The members of our AGs use appreciation to dissolve old resentments, attract new relationships with family and loved ones, get promotions, gain self-esteem, and improve physical well-being, as well as for a host of other uses that we describe in this book.

Our clients, friends, and AG members have taught us more about the life-altering power of appreciation than we could ever have discovered by ourselves. With their help, we have learned that appreciation is a remarkably effective way to bring out the best in yourself, the best in your life, and the best in those with whom you love, work, and play. Appreciation alters how you perceive and interpret what happens to you. This new outlook changes how you respond to events and situations, which in turn changes how the world and the people in it respond to you.

The appreciators we work with continually show us how appreciation opens up new possibilities for success, love, joy, and abundance, and convince us that appreciation benefits everyone who comes in contact with it. Appreciation has no downside; not only that, we've learned through hands-on experiences that appreciation functions as an attractor, drawing desired experiences to you—whether it's a terrific new job, a revitalized marriage, or increased health, energy, and well-being. It is with great joy—and profound appreciation—that we now share with you all that we've learned about the immense power of appreciation.

Noelle C. Nelson

Jeannine Lemare Calaba

Los Angeles, 2003

1

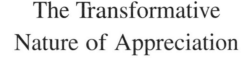

The Transformative
Nature of Appreciation

What Is Appreciation?

When you think of appreciation, what's the first thing that comes to mind? Probably something you're supposed to do, as in "Appreciate the roof over your head, some people don't have one," or something you failed to do, as in "You don't appreciate a thing I do for you!"

Most of us were subjected to such "appreciation-by-guilt," yelled by an irate parent with predictable regularity throughout our childhoods. If you have children, you may be doing the shouting yourself. As unpleasant as shouting or being shouted at may be, it tells you worlds about what appreciation really means.

When you're yelling "You don't appreciate a thing I do for you!" to your kids, what you mean is "You aren't grateful for what I do for you. You don't value what I do for you. You don't see its worth, how meaningful or important this thing I do for you is." The upshot is, you feel unappreciated.

You've probably felt unappreciated in much the same way by bosses, girlfriends, boyfriends, family members, husbands, wives, friends, lovers, coworkers—

just about anybody you have ever interacted with. The bottom line is that you feel what you're offering isn't valued by the person you're offering it to, and therefore he or she isn't grateful for it.

What happens when you do feel appreciated by that child, boss, lover, mother-in-law, or friend? Your spirits soar! You feel that you are important to that person; you feel competent and happy. Well, you have the same effect on others when you show your appreciation.

When you deliberately decide to appreciate people or things, you don't wish them harm and you don't do harm. Instead, you nurture, support, and love. As a result, they—and you—are transformed.

A New Definition of Appreciation

This book describes the transformative energy of consistent, proactive appreciation, which can propel your life from good to great, from troubled to joyous, from struggling to successful. By reading this book, you will learn about a kind of appreciation that can change your very approach to life and living.

You'll learn how to use this energy, which comes not from your usual duty-bound appreciation, not from your politically or socially correct appreciation, nor even from your heartfelt-but-soon-forgotten appreciation, but from a very different type of appreciation.

What kind of appreciation can transform your life? Appreciation that consists of two vital components: gratitude plus valuing. *It is this combination of gratitude and valuing that gives appreciation its power as a transformative energy.*

Gratitude

Gratitude is a receptive energy. It engages your heart. You feel or express gratitude after something pleasing has happened. A friend helps you out of trouble;

you are grateful. You notice the good things in your life; you are grateful. Most people are thinking of gratitude when they use the word "appreciation." Spiritual leaders, authors, and others—from the Dalai Lama to Louise Hay to Oprah Winfrey—have extolled the benefits of practicing gratitude through journals, meditation, and an "attitude of gratitude."

Valuing

The valuing aspect of appreciation is a dynamic energy; it engages your mind. When you value something or someone, you actively use your mind to think of it, why it matters to you, what it is worth to you. In the world of finance, when something appreciates, it grows in value. The same is true in the rest of our lives. A house is just a space until it is filled with the people and things that you cherish, and then it is a place called "home."

Because you choose what you think, you can deliberately select thoughts that value someone or something, rather than thoughts that devalue that person or thing. Consciously choosing to value the people and things in your life is what makes it possible for you to use appreciation *proactively*. You don't have to wait for something pleasing to happen in order to start valuing. You can choose to value someone or something before they have contributed anything at all to your life.

The act of proactively valuing transforms gratitude from an after-the-fact expression of feeling to a before-the-fact, deliberate engaging of energy. This is the energy of appreciation!

Appreciation as Energy

When you step outside the idea of appreciation as gratitude expressed after the fact, and start to think of appreciation as an *energy* you use proactively with intention, it's an entirely different experience. In this regard, appreciation can be likened to electricity. Electricity can be thought of as a simple tool: you flick a switch when you want light, as a response to the dark. Or, electricity can be thought of as an energy, which can be used as a source of power for any number of uses. So it is with appreciation. You can think of appreciation as a response to something you are grateful for, or you can think of appreciation as an energy, a source of *power* that can be harnessed, as electricity is, for any number of uses. A few examples:

- Use the power of appreciation to change your body's response to stress, and to encourage good health, an enhanced immune system, better energy, and faster healing.
- Use appreciation's power to increase your satisfaction and joy at home and at work, to improve your relationships and increase the love in your life, and to reduce conflict and support cooperation.
- Use appreciation to develop better self-esteem and self-confidence, and to better cope with change or crisis.
- Focus the energy of appreciation to attract abundance and success.
- Use the power of appreciation to attract new relationships (romantic and otherwise) into your life.

Appreciation used deliberately, purposefully, and proactively can transform almost any experience, no matter how challenging, into one you value and are grateful for. Mastering the energy of appreciation can rock your world. It can literally be magic for your life.

The Appreciators Group

In August 2001, we invited seven people to form an Appreciators Group (AG). We asked members to choose one thing in their lives that they wished to transform or attract. Over a period of six weeks, we taught them how to use appreciation to do so, using the techniques described in this book. One member wanted a better relationship with his adolescent daughter, who was acting out and refusing to talk to him. Another member had suffered a severe setback in her job; she wanted to use appreciation to dissolve her resentment over her downsized position and to help her get her career back on track. Yet another bemoaned the lack of love in her life and wanted to fill that void.

The results exceeded our expectations. Not only were all the members of the group successful, but they taught us a great deal more about the power of appreciation than we ourselves had been aware of. As Erin, a group member, told us:

"I've found that I can use appreciation as I do oxygen: to breathe life into my relationships and the goals I want to create for myself. If everyone did this, I believe that the impact on the world could be phenomenal—more love, less war, and more understanding."

Another AG member, Sylvia, says:

"Appreciation did a lot more than bring me a new relationship; it changed how I feel about myself and my life. There's a peace in my heart now, and this really deep security within, which is making everything in my life easier and better. I didn't expect that."

Since then, we have continued to work with Appreciators Groups, developing and refining our techniques. We are excited to share with you in the following chapters our methods for harnessing the energy of appreciation.

2

The Energy of 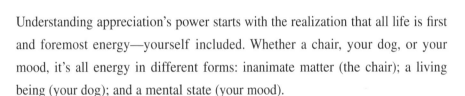 Appreciation

Understanding appreciation's power starts with the realization that all life is first and foremost energy—yourself included. Whether a chair, your dog, or your mood, it's all energy in different forms: inanimate matter (the chair); a living being (your dog); and a mental state (your mood).

All of this energy manifests as vibration, and that vibration can be measured in terms of frequency—the number of vibrations per second. Some vibrations are imperceptible, like the earth's rhythm (which is approximately 7.5 Hz, or 7.5 times per second, as described in Fabien Maman's *The Role of Music in the Twenty-First Century*). Other vibrations are easier to perceive, such as musical tones, which vibrate at 16–20,000 Hz. As Charles Taylor notes in *The Physics of Musical Sounds*, not only can we hear these tones, but we often actually feel them in our bodies.

(**Note:** Many of the practical concepts developed throughout this book, relative to vibrational attraction and the art of allowing, have been inspired by the works of the Abraham-Hicks Teachers, which can be found at www.abraham-hicks.com.)

You yourself have a frequency of vibration. This book has a frequency of vibration, as does the thought floating in the back of your mind, and your boss's nasty mood this morning. Everything, whether seemingly solid (living beings and inanimate objects) or immaterial (thoughts and feelings), has a frequency of vibration. The energy of appreciation is also expressed through its frequency of vibration.

Appreciation's Powerful Frequency of Vibration

The impact of appreciation's frequency of vibration is very powerful, as demonstrated by Dr. Masaru Emoto, who has researched the impact of thoughts, feelings, and music on the crystalline structure of water. In his book, *Messages from Water*, he and his team have photographed and examined, with a high-powered microscope, the crystalline formations of ice before and after exposure to different phenomena. For example, Dr. Emoto affixed the words "love and appreciation" to a test tube of water. The water was frozen and examined, then compared to water identical in all respects except that it had not been in the presence of the words. The results are startling, as shown in the photographs on page 19.

The first photograph (Figure 1) shows a randomly selected sample of crystals from distilled water. The crystalline shapes are relatively unformed, and have a nebulous or blurred quality.

The second photograph (Figure 2) shows an example from a random sampling of water crystals formed in the presence of the words "love and appreciation." The crystalline formation is well-defined, precise, complex, and beautifully lacy.

Then Dr. Emoto affixed to another test tube of water the words "You make me sick. I will kill you." As you can see from the third photograph (Figure 3), these words had a very different impact on the water's crystalline structure. Dr. Emoto describes this crystal as "distorted, imploded and dispersed." Its structure is chaotic, ill-defined, and has nothing in common with the pristine beauty of the "love and appreciation" crystal.

If the differing vibrational frequencies of words can have this enormous effect on the crystalline structure of water, imagine the impact on your life of a purposefully directed vibration of appreciation!

How could the presence of different words affect the very structure of water? If you consider that all things at their source are energy, and that all things can interact with each other at that level, such a phenomenon makes sense. (This interaction at the energetic level happens through the interplay of frequencies of vibration, as discussed by Valerie Hunt in *Infinite Mind: The Science of Human Vibrations*, and by Joel Sternheimer in his article "The Music of the Elementary Particles.")

Dr. Candace Pert's groundbreaking research in biochemistry demonstrates that emotions are vibratory in nature, and actually "connect the physical to the nonphysical." In *Molecules of Emotion*, she notes that this connection happens even at the cellular level, where receptor molecules vibrate, "dancing and rhythmically awaiting" the chemical messages that emotions bring.

Nowhere is the transformative power of appreciation more evident than at the level of our most basic functions: the beating of our hearts and the workings of our brains. Here, the impact of appreciation is unmistakable.

When you feel negative emotions (such as anger), your heart's rhythm is disordered, as shown in the graph on the next page from Doc Childre and Howard Martin's research in *The HeartMath Solution* (Figure 4). Notice how jagged, unpredictable, and fluctuating the heart wave is.

A chaotic or disordered heart rhythm creates a chain reaction in your body: your blood vessels constrict and your blood pressure rises. Eventually you may suffer from hypertension, which greatly increases your chances of heart disease and stroke.

Your Heart on Anger

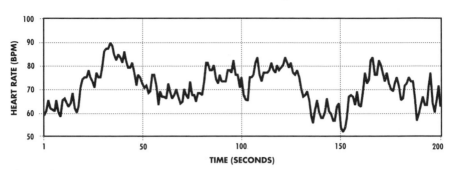

Figure 4.

As shown in the second graph (Figure 5; also from *The HeartMath Solution*), when you are feeling appreciation, your heart rhythm is expressed on the graph as a steady, even, and balanced wave. It is harmonious.

Your Heart on Appreciation

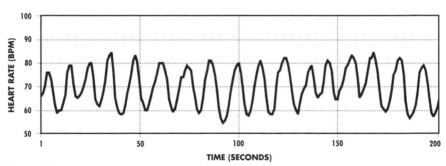

Figure 5.

Harmonious heart rhythms support good cardiovascular health. Your immune system is enhanced, your nervous system functions smoothly, and your hormonal balance is improved. Tom, a forty-year-old AG member, expressed how this worked for him:

When I get angry, I can feel my heart pounding. I get hot, and my whole body feels tight to where I'm shaking. I hardly needed my doctor to tell me I had high blood pressure. I really didn't expect appreciation to make any difference. I didn't even think about it, until my doctor asked me if I was doing anything different; on my last visit my blood pressure was way down, almost to normal. Then it dawned on me—yeah, I was doing something different all right. I was appreciating.

As Childre and Martin noted, in a state of sincere appreciation your whole body works synergistically to create an overall state of well being. Your energy is more buoyant and spirited. You feel better mentally, emotionally, and physically. Doreen, a twenty-seven-year-old AG member, had this to say: "I'm not as anxious as I used to be. I used to feel wired much of the time. My husband tells me I'm less edgy and nervous since I've been working with appreciation, and I must say, I feel a lot calmer, like my nerves have somehow smoothed out."

What you feel and think changes how your brain functions, which in turn immediately impacts how your mind operates—or doesn't. This phenomenon has been studied in depth by, among others, Dr. Daniel Amen in *Healing the Hardware of the Soul*, and Dr. M. S. George, whose study on the brain activity differences between sadness and happiness was reported in the American Journal of Psychiatry in 1995.

In his book, Dr. Amen, a psychiatrist and neuroscientist, states that our thoughts, feelings, and social behaviors impact directly upon our brain's capacity to function. Through the use of a neuro-imaging technique called the SPECT scan, he studies the correlation between blood flow patterns in the brain and the psychobehavioral symptoms we manifest. At the Amen Behavioral Clinic in Newport Beach, California, Dr. Amen assisted us in conducting a SPECT scan analysis to compare the visible differences in blood flow in the brain when we are experiencing negative or appreciative thoughts and feelings.

Figure 6 (page 20) shows a 3D image of what the blood flow to your brain is like when you are experiencing negative thoughts and feelings. The red color indicates areas in the brain where blood flow is occurring. Notice the overall diminished level of blood flow in this scan, particularly in the area of the cerebellum at the bottom of the image. Note also the indentation in blue at the right side of the image, which represents decreased activity in the left temporal cortex.

In our sessions with Dr. Amen, we learned that when you think negative thoughts, your cerebellum, which controls integrated movement, hardly functions at all. You experience physical difficulties and suffer from a lack of coordination. In the words of Dr. Amen, "You're like the baseball player who keeps striking out no matter how hard he tries not to." Your left temporal lobe, that part of your brain that keeps you on an even keel, doesn't receive enough blood flow. You become emotionally unstable and may experience anxiety or fear for no apparent reason. Your thoughts get jumbled and your memory is disrupted. You are more vulnerable to rage, dark thoughts, and violent actions. As a consequence of thinking negative thoughts, you feel angry, hostile, frustrated, distressed, anxious, and depressed, emotions that will lead you to respond with negative and destructive behaviors.

Figure 7 (page 21) shows a 3D picture of what the blood flow to your brain is like when you are experiencing appreciative thoughts and feelings. Compare the overall increase in blood flow here (i.e., the areas in red) with the negativity scan, particularly in the area of the cerebellum at the bottom of the image. Notice the rounded shape on the right side of the image where there was a blue indentation before, representing improved blood flow to the left temporal lobe. Also visible in this scan is an increase in blood flow to the cingulate gyrus (center top) and left basal ganglia (upper right side), areas of the brain that help us shift gears and maintain adaptability.

As Dr. Amen explained, when you think thoughts of appreciation, your brain functions well, firing on all cylinders, so to speak. Your cingulate gyrus and left basal ganglia are appropriately active, allowing you to be flexible, collaborative, and motivated to set goals. Your thoughts are clearly focused, and you can readily switch from one idea to another. Your memory is intact. Your cerebellum is innervated, and physically you are coordinated and energized. Your left temporal lobe operates fully, making you less susceptible to rage, violent actions, or dark thoughts.

Keith, an AG member, shares his experience:

I used to get real paranoid. I was not just waiting for the other shoe to drop. I was actively looking for it. I had a lot of trouble concentrating and it was hard for me to make decisions. I didn't know there was any other way to be! I thought being scared and worried all the time was normal, that feeling dispirited and out of sorts was just part of twenty-first-century life. I mean, look at the news! But the more I appreciate, the more I'm discovering that's not the way it's got to be. I'm not as worried, I don't panic at every little thing. I can think more clearly. I can make decisions without torturing myself over them. I still have my days, that's for sure, but it's like I'm coming out of a fog that I didn't even know was there!

When you think appreciative thoughts, you feel uplifted, happy, joyous, enthusiastic, and at peace, which will lead you to respond with behaviors corresponding to these positive feelings. Donna, another AG member, says, "Sometimes I have a hard time relating to me then and me now. My friends tease me, they call me 'Ms. Bubbly' and want to know where I hid 'Ms. Bitchy.' I'm more upbeat, excited about things—happier, I guess. I know I'm nicer to people; heck, I'm even nicer to myself."

Entrainment

The impact of appreciation is unmistakable, but how does it work? How does appreciation vibrationally interact with your heart or your brain? Although the biochemistry is complex, we can best understand this interaction through the principle of entrainment.

Entrainment is the process whereby one frequency of vibration aligns with or matches another. For example, when the frequency of vibration of a singer's voice matches the frequency of vibration of a crystal glass, the glass may shatter. If two violin strings tuned to the same pitch are at rest across a room from each other, and one violin string is bowed, the string across the room will begin to vibrate at the same pitch (frequency) as the bowed string.

The phenomenon of entrainment was discovered quite accidentally by Christian Huygens in the seventeenth century. Huygens was the inventor of the pendulum clock, and owned a large collection of them. One day he noticed that all the pendulums were swinging in unison, which baffled him, since he had not set them to do so. He then deliberately set the pendulums swinging at different rhythms, only to find that they soon once again began to swing in perfect synchronization, led by the pendulum with the strongest rhythm.

Entrainment explains how your heart rhythms align your brain waves to them. As the authors of *The HeartMath Solution* state, when we're in a deep state of appreciation, our brain waves come into harmony with our heart rhythms (precisely at 0.1 Hz, the point at which our heart rhythms complete one cycle every ten seconds).

In Figure 8, the graphs on the left show real-time recordings of a person's heart rhythms and brain waves while experiencing a feeling of sincere appreciation. The large spikes in the graphs on the right show where the heart rhythms and brain waves have synchronized, or come into harmony, at 0.1 Hz.

Head-Heart Entrainment

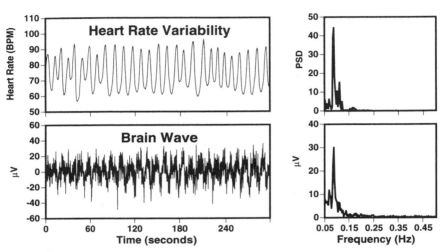

Figure 8.

Entrainment explains many phenomena that might otherwise seem mystifying. For example, if you walk into a room of depressed people, sure enough, after a while, you're depressed. Or if you walk into a room of happy, laughing people who invite you to join them, you soon feel happier. In both cases, you've experienced entrainment.

Given that the collective vibration of a roomful of people is generally stronger than your individual frequency, your vibration will be entrained to their vibration. Their collective vibration harmonizes with the portion of your vibration that may be even latently depressed or cheerful, and "pulls" you toward a vibration of depression or cheerfulness, unless you actively resist it.

However, you can't entrain what isn't there. If all your thoughts and feelings are angry ones, and no frequency of vibration of happiness exists within you, then a potentially happy experience will not lift your spirits. There is nothing in you with which a frequency of vibration of happiness can align, therefore nothing for it to entrain.

When people say "Don't try to cheer me up," they are reflecting this. They are in essence saying, "I have no frequency of vibration of cheer within me." All the cheering-up energy you may send in their direction will be to no avail.

Have you ever said, "You make me mad," or "She makes me feel great"? Most of us walk around in vibrational "neutral" most of the time. We're not deliberately focusing our thoughts or feelings, we're just letting them ramble. This is why it feels like people or situations can "make" you feel a certain way. What's really happening is that in the absence of your own strongly focused vibration, you are being entrained by another person's or situation's vibration. Their strongly focused vibration simply aligns proportionately with that part of your frequency of vibration that is even weakly similar to theirs, and sure enough, you end up feeling very differently.

Conversely, entrainment explains why when you deliberately respond to a situation with a powerfully focused energy, you will be responded to in kind, if no resistance is present. Familiar phrases such as "like attracts like," "what goes around, comes around," and "what you give is what you get" reflect this scientific reality. We live in a universe composed of vibrating energy, so whatever energy you give off—such as the energy of appreciation—will support and encourage experiences of like energy.

To prove the truth of "what you give is what you get," try the following experiment that Peter Tompkins described in *The Secret Life of Plants*. Plant identical seedlings in three different pots with an identical amount and type of potting soil in each pot. Place the pots side by side, so the three plants receive the same light. Feed and water all three plants identical amounts. The only variance in their treatment is that you will talk to each plant differently.

To the first plant, say only appreciative things, such as, "What a wonderful little seedling you are. Look at how delicate your new leaves are, how strongly your little roots hold to the earth."

To the second, say nothing.

To the third, say only mean and unappreciative things, such as, "What a pathetic excuse for a seedling you are. You're disgusting. You're not worth the earth I planted you in."

Over time, the appreciated plant will grow healthy and strong, the neutral plant will grow fairly well, and the unappreciated plant will be stunted and fare poorly. Like truly does attract like.

As you respond to people and events with appreciation, and thus entrain more positive experiences, your life becomes happier. As you become happier, appreciating becomes easier—especially when you realize that appreciating is what brought you this happiness in the first place. The direct and unmistakable consequence of appreciation is happiness.

Greg, an AG member, says, "Appreciating seems to expand on itself and gain momentum. The more I use it, the more I find myself spontaneously doing so—and the more opportunities seem to come my way for using it."

His Holiness the Dalai Lama, in *The Art of Happiness*, notes, "I believe that the very purpose of our life is to seek happiness. That is clear. Whether one believes in religion or not, whether one believes in this religion or that religion, we all are seeking something better in life. So, I think, the very motion of our life is towards happiness."

In the next chapter, you'll see how you can use the energy of appreciation in your search for happiness in life. You'll discover the benefits of appreciating proactively, and learn how to appreciate most effectively to receive those benefits.

Vibrational Effects on the Crystalline Structures of Water

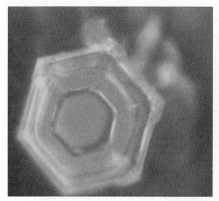

Masaru Emoto

Figure 1. Distilled Water

Masaru Emoto

Figure 2. Appreciation

Masaru Emoto

Figure 3. "You make me sick. I will kill you."

Your Brain on Negativity

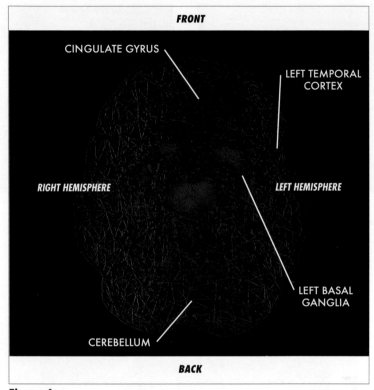

Figure 6.

SPECT study measuring blood flow to the brain while experiencing negative thoughts and feelings.

Underside view of the brain

Your Brain on Appreciation

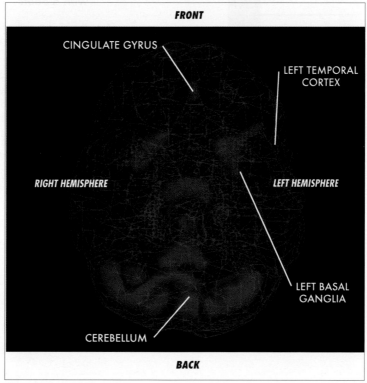

Figure 7.

SPECT study measuring blood flow to the brain while experiencing appreciative thoughts and feelings.

Underside view of the brain

BIODOTS

Color approximations and general interpretations of stress:

Violet 94.6°F. - Very relaxed

Blue 93.6°F. - Calm

Turquoise 92.6°F. - Relaxing

Green 91.6°F - Involved (mml)

Yellow 90.6°F. - Unsettled

Amber 89.6°F - Tense

Black 87°F. - Very Tense

Work Your "Appreciation Muscle" with Biodots

1. Place the biodot in the dip between your thumb and forefinger.

2. Relax, breathe deeply, and think and feel thoughts of appreciation until your biodot turns green or teal.

3. Keep your biodot at that green or teal level by actively thinking and feeling appreciation.

3

Becoming an Appreciator

Appreciation is most powerful when it ceases to be something that you do only occasionally, and instead becomes your basic approach to life. When appreciation becomes the lens through which you view living, you can reap its incalculable benefits.

You must first be willing to overcome certain resistances to appreciating, those reasons you give yourself for why you shouldn't have to appreciate in a particular situation, or why it won't work, or how appreciation is just too hard in this or that circumstance. As Earl, an AG member tells us, "The hardest thing for me was to be willing to appreciate someone when they're not appreciating me. I thought 'Why should I be the one to make the effort—she's not.' It took me a long time to get over that." You have to be willing to change patterns of thinking and feeling that may stand in the way of your being a full-time, hands-on, "this is how I do life no matter what" appreciator. You cannot use the power of appreciation only when it is convenient.

It's not easy. Our first and most automatic reactions are often antithetical to the appreciator's way: we want to blame, deny, lash out, avoid—anything but appreciate. As one member of an Appreciators Group noted, "It was really hard at first, not to use hatred as a motivation anymore."

But if you want to enjoy the full range of appreciation's benefits, you must release negative patterns of thinking and feeling, and replace them with appreciative ones. You must be willing to take the high road.

Appreciation Is the High Road

Appreciation takes courage and considerable resolve. It's the high road, and not everyone is willing to take it. Let's face it, when you choose thoughts of valuing and gratitude as your primary way of being, you are turning off the road well traveled. You are saying no to blame, to resentment, to revenge, to violence in any form—from bad-mouthing others, to kicking the dog, to berating a person. You are saying no to victimhood, to martyrdom, to passing the buck, to criticism, and to demeaning yourself or others.

When you choose appreciation, you are saying yes to being your own best friend without becoming narcissistically self-centered, yes to seeing the best in others without being blind to their weaknesses, yes to perceiving the greatest possible good in all situations while being alert to what will and won't work for you. You are willing to stand up for yourself. You are willing to recognize and applaud what's good about yourself, what's good about others, and what's good about your life.

Appreciation takes discernment, forbearance, and just plain guts. The good news is, it's doable, because everyone—without exception—is capable of appreciating, of finding value, of being grateful.

There is something you are grateful for right now. What is it? To see how gratitude functions in your life right now, take a moment to complete the following test, developed by psychologist Robert A. Emmons and researchers at Southern Methodist University, as described in their article, "The Grateful Disposition: A Conceptual and Empirical Topography."

The Gratitude Questionnaire

Circle the number beside each statement that indicates how much you agree with the statement. (Note that the numbers for statements E and F reverse the order.)

1 = strongly disagree

2 = disagree

3 = slightly disagree

4 = neutral

5 = slightly agree

6 = agree

7 = strongly agree

_____ A. I have so much in life to be thankful for.

   1 2 3 4 5 6 7

_____ B. If I had to list everything I felt grateful for, it would be a very long list.

   1 2 3 4 5 6 7

_____ C. I am grateful to a wide variety of people.

   1 2 3 4 5 6 7

_____ D. As I get older, I find myself more able to appreciate the people, events, and situations that have been part of my life history.

   1 2 3 4 5 6 7

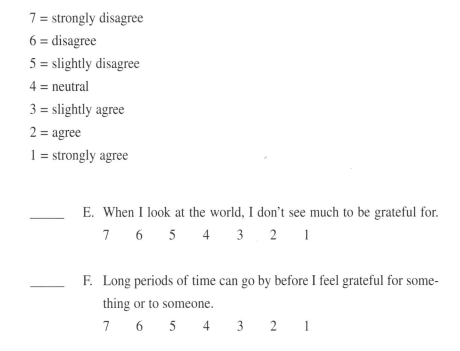

7 = strongly disagree

6 = disagree

5 = slightly disagree

4 = neutral

3 = slightly agree

2 = agree

1 = strongly agree

_____   E. When I look at the world, I don't see much to be grateful for.

                  7   6   5   4   3   2   1

_____   F. Long periods of time can go by before I feel grateful for something or to someone.

                  7   6   5   4   3   2   1

Now add up your scores for all six items. This number should be between six and forty-two. (Remember, for statements E and F, the numbers are reversed.) The higher your score, the more likely you are to be feeling gratitude.

Dr. Emmons notes, "Compared to their less grateful counterparts, grateful people are higher in positive emotions and life satisfaction, and lower in negative emotions such as depression, anxiety, and envy. They also appear to be more socially oriented—they are more empathic, forgiving, helpful and supportive than are their less grateful counterparts."

No matter what your current level of gratitude, you can increase and develop your ability to appreciate. Let's start by overcoming those resistances we mentioned earlier in the chapter.

Facing Resistance

Even when you commit to the practice of appreciation, you're going to find reasons not to appreciate in this or that circumstance, and you're going to concoct rationalizations for why you don't think you should have to appreciate, or why it's downright impossible, in certain situations. On your journey to becoming an appreciator, these resistances are like so many dragons you must face and slay.

Teresa, an AG member, notes, "What's going to happen when people start appreciating and start manifesting more of whatever it is they desire—dreams, love, visions—is that they are going to tap into their resistances and it's going to seem like, at times, it's getting worse instead of better. From the very beginning of this group I have felt resistances on different levels and worked through them. And I think that's very important, that people know that they are going to feel resistances."

Most forms of resistance come under one of three headings:

- "You first."
- "You just don't get it."
- "Oh my gosh, it's getting worse."

Overcoming "You First" Resistance

It's very hard to appreciate someone when they are standing there, pig-headed in their righteousness, absolutely unwilling to concede the least little point. It takes immense force of character, when something is truly not your fault, to set aside all thoughts of blame and deliberately go about the business of appreciating. Your whole being cries out: "Why should I have to be the one to do the appreciating? They caused this; it's their fault, not mine. Where's the justice in this? They should go first. They should admit their responsibility and appreciate me."

In a perfect world, they would indeed do that. In this wonderful but imperfect world, however, you may have to wait a very long time—a lifetime, in fact, and that may still not suffice—for some people to get off their righteousness, take responsibility for their actions, and appreciate you.

Rather than wait an eternity before you enjoy the benefits of appreciation, recognize that "you first" is simply a resistance. Once you see yourself feeling this way, just step away from your righteousness, however justified, and start rooting around for those appreciative thoughts and feelings.

What matters is not who's right, what matters is how happy you can be. Appreciation will never vindicate you, but appreciation will flood you with happiness. The choice is yours.

Overcoming "You Just Don't Get It" Resistance

Another resistance to appreciation is "you just don't get it," sometimes expressed as, "This is a terrible situation, I can't feel appreciation here!"

Indeed, you may be faced with a truly awful situation, but that doesn't mean that appreciation has no place in it. On the contrary, appreciation is a powerful tool that you can use to work your way through crisis to a better place.

What often gets in your way with this form of resistance are your feelings. You may be feeling anger, rage, humiliation, shame, shock, fear, or despair. You may feel depressed and completely unmotivated. It may be very difficult to set aside these feelings. You may believe that the situation will have to change before your feelings can change, but—as with wanting someone else to "go first"—waiting for a situation to change may mean a very long wait.

There is no need to endure such pain. The solution is simple, but sometimes seems so hard. If you can summon up just one small, appreciative thought (without denying your feelings, because appreciation is not denial), you're on your way to transforming the situation. When you do this, the results are intense.

Overcoming "Oh My Gosh, It's Getting Worse" Resistance

When you first begin working with appreciation, it may seem like the situation is getting worse, or not budging at all. The first thing to happen when you begin to appreciate a loved one in the midst of a troubled relationship may be that more arguments ensue. Your thought may be, "This appreciation stuff doesn't work. Forget it."

When this happens, remember the saying, "When the going gets tough, the tough get going," and use the techniques and skills you'll learn in this book to keep working on your appreciation. The increase in arguments may provide opportunities for greater clarification of issues. Your glaring differences may push you into therapy together, which will have beneficial effects. When you find the resolve to commit to appreciating no matter what, you have conquered one of the most challenging resistances.

Now that you're aware of the resistances you may encounter along the way, how do you become an appreciator? You start by appreciating life itself.

Appreciate Life

When you perceive and interpret people and events through the lens of appreciation, you increase the potential for good possibilities in your life. As Steven Covey notes in *The Seven Habits of Highly Effective People*, you become "opportunity-minded" as opposed to "problem-minded." Once you begin to use the power of appreciation, more things, people, and situations to appreciate make their way to you. You find today very good indeed, and look forward to a tomorrow full of even more joy. As Dr. Emmons writes in his article "The Joy of Thanks," "My colleagues and I are finding that gratitude, which we define as a felt sense of wonder, thankfulness, and appreciation for life, is more than simply a pleasant emotion to experience or a polite sentiment to express. It is, or at least can be, a basic disposition, one that seems to make lives happier, healthier, more fulfilling—and even longer."

Start by noticing what your current level of life-appreciation is. You can easily figure this out by listening to what you say when someone asks, "How are you? How's your day going?"

Is your reply something along the lines of, "Oh, you know, the usual. Another day, another dollar. Boy, that traffic was a bear—I couldn't believe it took me an hour to get to my last appointment. Oh, and what a pain in the butt he was. Wanted me to look at this, and explain that, just a royal pain."

Or is it more like, "Fine, thanks. I was lucky—I got to my appointment in time, even though traffic was heavy. My last appointment cracked me up. What a character! Wanted to know every last detail of what I was doing and why."

The second response expresses an optimistic and appreciative view of life. Both responses acknowledge the traffic and the "picky" nature of the last appointment. In an appreciative state of mind, you don't deny reality, you just choose to perceive and interpret it in a positive or appreciative manner. You choose to see the benefits to you in the events and people that come your way, and you are thankful for them. This does not mean that you never get angry, sad, or disappointed. You do, but you work through your negative emotions and return to a generally appreciative way of thinking and feeling.

Develop an Appreciative State of Mind

Try thinking appreciative and pessimistic thoughts at the same time. It doesn't work. You can't simultaneously think, "I value and am grateful for all the opportunities my life affords me," and, "Life sucks." It's more than a contradiction in terms, it's a *contradiction in vibration.*

As an optimist, you automatically see life as inherently good and worth living. You believe in the best possible outcome, and emphasize the most positive aspects of any situation.

Optimists thrive. As Dr. Martin Seligman states in *Learned Optimism*, research shows that optimists do better at work, school, and sports, and they tend to be healthier, live longer, and age well. Optimists recover from setbacks more quickly, are less likely to become depressed, and do better than predicted by aptitude tests—they actually outshine their own talents! When optimists run for office, they are more likely to win.

So, when you adopt an appreciative mindset, you set the stage for a great deal more. Appreciation is optimism maximized.

How do you step into an appreciative state of mind? The key is to consistently choose thoughts and feelings that express your valuing of people or situations. Choose not to entertain negative or devaluing thoughts and feelings. At first, many of your thoughts may not be appreciative; old habits die hard. Even people who have been practicing the power of appreciation find it difficult. Erin, an AG member, says, "Sometimes I can't stay in my appreciative state long enough. Maybe I'm there 60 percent of the time. I'd like to aim for 100 percent. There are so many areas of my life that I need to bring appreciation to. It's a whole new rebirth for me."

Fortunately, over time, choosing appreciative thoughts and feelings becomes second nature. Here's how Sandra, an AG member, describes her experience:

> I used to walk around with a "woe is me" attitude, for pretty much everything from traffic jams to a fight with my mom to a pain-in-the-neck boss. So when my boyfriend dumped me, that's the first place I went. It never occurred to me that his dumping me actually got me out of a relationship I was miserable in, until I started looking for things to appreciate.

But it didn't happen overnight. I started with the little things, like appreciating the time I used to waste cursing out freeway gridlock as time to listen to a good book on tape. Eventually I got my "woe is me"–to–appreciation ratio down from 100 to 1, to about 70–30. By that point, instead of dwelling morosely on being dumped, I was able to get over it and get on with my life. I have a way to go, but I feel a lot happier heading in this direction. And I'm starting to feel good about myself—that's opening up a whole new world for me.

Another member, Pete, explained his process this way:

I've always been a grateful person, but I never did it on purpose. If something nice happened, I was grateful—big deal. So, learning to appreciate my first cup of coffee in the morning, the ride-share that gets me to work, my supervisor (whether she's in a good mood or not), my job—the whole nine yards, on purpose—was completely new to me. I had to put post-its up everywhere to remember to do it. I even set my watch alarm to buzz every hour so I'd remember to stop and appreciate something, until that got too annoying. But I kept working at it, because I started to feel more motivated, and just sort of generically happier about everything. I noticed people helping me more, being nice to me a lot, good things happening. I started to keep kind of a journal of this stuff, to remind me when I'm feeling lazy or ornery or just not in the mood, how very worthwhile it is to deliberately appreciate.

If you listen carefully to yourself, you may find that the main obstacle to an appreciative state of mind is an unconscious undercurrent of complaining, worrying, and "what if"-ing that surfaces any time you're not actively thinking of something else. Here's an example:

> I can't believe I forgot to shut the bathroom window. I'm such an idiot, the cat got out, it's my fault and my husband is going to kill me. Where's the darn cleaner anyway? I thought it was on this street. What if they've moved? What if I can't find them? Oh, please! Watch where you're going! Cell-phone driver, naturally. Where is that darn cleaner? I'm going to be late for work. I wonder if that sale is still on at the shoe store. With my luck, they'll be all out of my size. Why do I have to wear a size 6 anyway? Another red light. Rats!

Most of the time, you're not even aware of such thoughts going on. And they do go on—and on and on, until you finally nod off, and even after that, worrisome thoughts can wake you up in the middle of the night or pop up in your dreams.

Transform your negative thoughts into more appreciative thoughts by actively countering each negative thought with more positive reflections. Using the preceding example, each negative thought is countered by a positive response (in italics) in the following:

> I can't believe I forgot to shut the bathroom window. I'm such an idiot, the cat got out...
>
> *Well, I'm not really such an idiot, it's natural for the cat to want to go out, she's done that before. And the cat has always found her way back, so she'll probably be there when we get home. I can appreciate her sense of "home."*
>
> Where's the darn cleaner anyway? I thought it was on this street. What if they've moved? What if I can't find them?

Well, it's not likely that they've moved. And if they have, I can always ask my friends who they use. I'm thankful for my friends. I'll make one more pass around the block and let it go for now.

Oh, please! Watch where you're going! Cell-phone driver, naturally.

Whew—I'm grateful for my good reactions. And cell phones aren't bad in and of themselves—I certainly appreciate mine.

Where is that darn cleaner? I'm going to be late for work.

Nope, I'm not going to be late for work. I appreciate that I already decided to let the cleaner go for now—it's not worth being late for work.

I wonder if that sale is still on at the shoe store...

I'm grateful that they're having one! Maybe on the way home I can check it out.

Another red light...

Not a problem, I remember this is a short one.

Choosing appreciative thoughts is a conscious process. As you persist, you'll find that your negative thoughts are highly repetitive, and as such are relatively easy to spot and change.

As you practice choosing thoughts of appreciation, also pay attention to your spoken words. Do you complain a lot? What do you complain about? Do you dwell on what is going wrong, or is unpleasant, inconvenient, or worrisome? How much do you focus on what is going right, or is pleasant, easy, and reassuring?

Keep in mind that most situations have positive and negative aspects. Whenever you find yourself complaining or dwelling on what you don't like, switch your focus quickly to what you do appreciate. Practice noticing, thinking, and talking about the aspects of the situation that you can value and be grateful for.

Switching your focus doesn't mean that there aren't things in your life that need fixing. If you uncover something in your complaining that does require attention, jot it down so that you can take care of it without having to carry it around in your mind where it can interfere with your ability to appreciate life.

Play the Appreciation Game

Notice that appreciating isn't a matter of using the exact words "I appreciate" or "I am grateful for" or "thank you." Appreciating is less a matter of the literal words you use and more a matter of intent. When you are looking to find things to value and be grateful for in any given situation, you are appreciating, whatever your precise words.

Make a game of appreciating. Deliberately think about the many things you can appreciate about every facet of your current life. No matter where you are, or what you are doing, practice appreciating.

Remember the car game called "Spot the License Plate"? Well, now you can play "Spot Something to Appreciate"—whether you're on the road or off. Here's how it goes: You are sitting in gridlocked traffic on the freeway. What is there to appreciate?

- There is a road—without it, you couldn't get from point A to point B.
- No matter how dreadful the gridlock, at some point it will loosen up and you will be on your way.
- You have a radio, tape deck, or CD player to listen to, and you can enjoy music, an audiobook, or other people's opinions. In the absence of all three of these, you can enjoy thinking about things you don't usually take the time to think about, whether that's how to decorate your dream home, or the nature of existence.

- There is a sky above you, blue and clear, or gray and wet, each of which has its beauty.
- There are plants, buildings, or something else along the road about which you can find things to appreciate. The very fact that trees and other plants can grow by the side of the freeway is something to appreciate.

Let's try another one. You are standing in an overly long line at the checkout counter in the grocery store. Your feet hurt, you want to get home, and the new cashier is taking forever to scan items. What is there to appreciate?

- There is a well-stocked store close to home. Even if it takes a while to get through the line, you've found everything you need for tonight's dinner.
- You're safe and warm (or cool and dry) as you wait.
- There are people in front of and behind you that you can chat with, and who knows, it might be a very interesting conversation.
- You have some private time to think or to lightly close your eyes and enjoy a few minutes of hassle-free drifting.

That's how to play the Appreciation Game. It's a lot more fun than standing there bemoaning your aching feet, which will never make them hurt any less.

Opportunities to appreciate in everyday life are limited only by your willingness to see them.

Appreciate Yourself

As you continue using the power of appreciation, turn from the broad goal of appreciating life to the more intimate need to appreciate yourself. When you appreciate yourself, you bring out what's best within yourself. Dan, an AG member, sums up his experience: "Through appreciation, I am really finding myself again—which is a great feeling. I'm stronger, more confident. The strength comes from rediscovering myself."

Who better can appreciate you than yourself? It just won't do to wait until someone else comes along to do it for you (remember the "you first" resistance?). That won't happen until you appreciate yourself. Develop and deepen your appreciation of yourself by exploring what you value about yourself, and the gratitude that flows from that valuing.

Mouthing an empty "I love me" won't work. It takes more than that. You have to identify the specific qualities and attributes that make up who you are, cherish them, and feel a deep sense of gratitude for them. Here's a simple way to consciously appreciate your unique self:

Take a sheet of paper and draw a vertical line down the middle. On the left side, list the inner qualities and traits you value about yourself. On the right side, write down why you are grateful for each one of these qualities and traits.

At first, you may feel that there is not all that much to appreciate about yourself. Not so! There is a great deal to appreciate about each and every one of us. If, however, you are having a tough time coming up with something, think what friends or family have said about you over the years. Think about what you're good at and what inner traits are revealed by that. Ask yourself what coworkers like about you. Think about the qualities you appreciate in your friends—these will often be the qualities that you possess yourself.

Here are some examples, just to get you started. You may think of yourself as a pretty smart person; write that down. How about your sense of humor? Do you interact easily with others? If so, write it down. Do you value your sense of design and proportion? Or is it the wonderful relationship you have with animals? Is your common sense something you value about yourself? How about your ability to fix almost anything? Maybe it's your appreciation for art? Your love of sports? What about your deep concern for your family? Your ability to grasp world affairs? Or do you value your skill with video games and all things mechanical?

Now it's time to address the right side of the paper. Ask yourself why you are grateful for each of your qualities; for example, "Why am I grateful for my intelligence?" Be specific. You might be grateful for your intelligence because it helps you earn your living. You might be grateful for your ability to think well because it helps you solve problems effectively. You might be grateful for your intelligence because it helps you understand football plays or the nuances of foreign films.

It's important to write down the specific reasons that your individual strengths and character traits are important to you. This makes it much easier for you to fully and genuinely appreciate yourself!

As you value your qualities and are grateful for them, you recognize the value of who you are. As you appreciate yourself, you become more of who you really are: vibrant, enthusiastic, and confident.

Cleaning Up Your Personal Vibration

Appreciating yourself is not to be confused with being arrogant. Arrogant people spend their time comparing themselves to others, judging themselves to be better than everyone else, and finding all others lacking. Appreciating yourself has nothing to do with other people. It is purely between you and yourself. When you work on honestly appraising and being grateful for your individual gifts, you are neither immodest nor full of yourself. You are simply cleaning up your personal vibration, much as you might clean up an attic, a stock portfolio, or your sock drawer.

Cleaning up your personal vibration means weeding out negative beliefs about yourself. Negative beliefs, which get in the way of developing your appreciative vibration, generally fall into three categories:

- Putting yourself down: "I'm not talented," "I never get things right," or "I'll never be successful at anything."
- Feeling sorry for yourself, taking the role of a victim: "Poor me, I can't be (or do or have) that," "Nobody loves me," or "Nobody appreciates me."
- Being self-critical, distorting your self-image so that it includes only your flaws or perceived flaws, and exaggerating those flaws: "I'm boring (or stupid, lazy, unimaginative, etc.)."

As you explore your qualities and begin to value and be grateful for them, many of your negative beliefs and opinions about yourself will simply drop off. If you still find yourself making self-deprecating statements, stop, and consciously take a moment to change your negative beliefs into positive statements. The table on the next page gives some examples that show how you can change your outlook by consciously finding a way to appreciate even unpleasant situations.

Self-appreciation is a powerful antidote to unhappiness. It frees you of the negative interpretations that act as chains, binding you to miserable experiences, and it empowers you to take positive action and move into more satisfying situations.

Rick, an AG member, tells us:

We'd been saving up for a down payment on a house. Our kids were getting older and our apartment was just too crowded. So finally we got it together, found a great house in a good neighborhood that wasn't way out of our budget, and then the loan fell through. My credit wasn't good enough to offset the fact that we're both self-employed.

I was just miserable. I kept thinking, "What a loser I am, I can't even put my family in a decent home. I'm a terrible husband, I'm a pathetic father. I've failed my kids, let down my wife." I was in the self-esteem toilet.

Situation	Negative Belief	Positive Statement
You get laid off.	*I'm not talented.*	*The company's been having problems lately. It needed to downsize and my position had to go.*
Your lover leaves you.	*Nobody loves me. I'm unlovable.*	*Some people are better matched than others. We had our good times. We just didn't fit together well enough to be a "forever" couple.*
Your ideas are shot down or not taken seriously at a company meeting.	*I'm not creative. I'm stupid.*	*I don't think I've understood what this company's needs and objectives are yet. I need to spend some more time looking at what ideas have been implemented in the past.*

My wife said, "Well, why don't you try doing some of that appreciation stuff you've been learning?" and the first thing that shot out of my mouth was, "Like that's gonna get us a loan?"

My wife ignored that comment, bless her heart, and pointed out how much I'd been beating up on myself lately, so I thought, OK, I'll start with un-beating myself through appreciation.

I got out a piece of paper and started writing down how I felt about myself, and then started working on finding some appreciation somewhere. I realized I'm not the first person to get turned down for a loan. That doesn't make me a loser, it just makes me "he-who-has-no-loan." I realized I was still working, still pulling in the bucks, still paying rent. My kids still loved me, so I figured I wasn't that bad a dad. I thought about how my wife was standing by me and telling me, "We're in this together." I could appreciate all of that about myself. So I wrote all this out, and I made myself read it over every day, appreciating as much as I could. I began feeling more confident, like it wasn't the end of the world and that I was still a capable guy. I could handle this. Then I heard an ad on the radio for "cleaning up your credit" and I thought, "Heck, it's worth a call." Well, what they had to say made sense to me. I took their advice, appreciated the heck out of it, and then gathered up my courage and went back to the bank. To my amazement, the bank was willing to work with me this time, and we were able to find (and finance!) another house that fit our needs. I knew this wasn't about luck or anything else like that. I knew I dug my way out of my "loser" hole by appreciating, and that appreciating myself started a whole new ball game. And I've been appreciating ever since.

By appreciating yourself, you dramatically alter how you perceive and interpret other people's behavior. Your more appreciative outlook generates positive responses from others. Instead of interpreting events by worrying—"Did I do it right or wrong?" "Do they like me or not?" or "Do they approve of me or not?"—you are free to interpret them more objectively, which immediately increases the range of your responses. Free of the need for others' regard, you have more to give to people and situations. Everybody likes to be valued by others, but when you appreciate yourself, you're not as needy for others to do so; you're not dependent on others for your self-esteem.

When a problem arises, if you appreciate yourself, you can look at what others might offer to the solution, rather than looking for someone to blame or criticize. You can perceive answers, pieces of the puzzle and possible solutions that might otherwise elude you.

When you appreciate yourself, people respond positively to your self-confidence and self-assurance. You are more likely to be entrusted with important projects or responsibility. Your likelihood of success in all areas of life automatically increases.

Alyne, an AG member, shares her experience:

I really wanted this promotion at work. I wanted it so bad, I could taste it, and I worked my butt off for it, jumping though all the hoops and connecting with all the right people. And one day—Hurrah! I got it.

Then it hit me: What if I couldn't handle the job? What if I didn't have the skills, the abilities, couldn't perform the way everybody expected? I was worrying myself right into failing miserably at it, and then I thought, "Wait a minute, if they gave me the position, I can't be all that incompetent. I must have something on the ball," and from there I started deliberately appreciating myself—appreciating the specific skills and abilities I had that could be valuable in this new position, like my resourcefulness, my creativity, my directness, my persistence, my enthusiasm for a job well done.

Well, appreciating myself put me in a very different frame of mind. I realized, "I don't have to do this alone, I can ask for help," so I went to my department head and said, "I want to do a bang-up, first-class job for you in my new position. Tell me what that will take." And she did! Not only that, but she virtually mentored me through the next six months until I was up and running on my own. Later she told me she was surprised and impressed by my courage in coming to her, that it told her I had what it took to make it in the company. It sure was nice to have my self-appreciation not only work for me, but also to have myself appreciated back in this way.

Deepen Your Appreciation of Others

Appreciating yourself makes it much easier to take the next step toward the power of appreciation: appreciating others. Since appreciation consists of valuing plus gratitude, feeling appreciation for another arises from consciously recognizing that person's value and then elucidating specific reasons why you are grateful for him or her.

When you value others, think about what you cherish about them, what you hold dear about them, what makes them important to you, and why they matter. When you're grateful for others, you're thankful that they exist, and you're pleased by their presence in your life. Spend time thinking about why you value and are grateful for someone you love, someone you can appreciate almost automatically, like a spouse or best friend. Because that appreciation comes so easily, it's a great place from which to practice your appreciation of others.

The Feelings of Appreciation

Think about how you value your best friend. What makes this friend so important to you? Write down all that you appreciate about your best friend.

Can you sense how good you feel when you're appreciating? Can you feel how relaxed you have become? How at peace you feel? How a smile plays around your face? How very pleasurable it is for you to be in this state of appreciation? Let yourself become familiar with this feeling, for it will tell you when you are truly appreciating someone else. Emotions are a great guide to what's truly happening inside you.

For others to feel the impact of your appreciation, however, your feeling it isn't enough. You must be able to express your appreciation, verbally and nonverbally.

The Language of Appreciation

For some people, expressing appreciation is natural and easy; for others, it is unfamiliar. It can be challenging to find the words. If that's true for you, try using some of the following examples as models to help you get started.

- Thanks so much for listening to me. I appreciate how you're always there for me.
- How thoughtful of you to remember that I like spicy food! Thank you!
- You're so good at reminding me of the important things in life—I am grateful.
- Your phone call picked me up right when I needed it most. I'm grateful.
- I'm really touched by your sharing your thoughts and feelings with me— thank you.
- Thanks for a fun evening together. I enjoy spending time with you.

If you're not used to verbally expressing appreciation, you may find that saying such things feels awkward at first. Cara, an AG member, said,

When I first started expressing my appreciation, I felt so weird. All I could come up with was, "Thank you for . . ."—you know, like a pat phrase I'd use over and over: "Thank you for being my friend," "thank you for talking with me about my work problem," "thank you for telling me the story of that movie you saw." It felt very stilted. Even when I had a lot to be grateful for, and a lot that I valued, I couldn't come up with the words. I felt like such a boob. Plus, I literally had to remind myself to do it.

So I made a pact with myself to say I appreciated something at least three times any time I got together with my best friend. I couldn't believe how hard it was to come up with three things when I was having a terrific time with my best friend, who I really do think the world of, and who in my heart I appreciate enormously. The words just wouldn't come even though I felt appreciation like crazy.

Now, of course, it's wonderfully easy, and I do it all the time without even thinking about it. But I still remember how uncomfortable it was to do it in the beginning!

Appreciation without Words

Have you ever seen a mother look at her newborn? There is wonder in her eyes as she delights in every particle of her baby's being: every finger, every hair, every coo. She holds her baby carefully, tenderly, with reverence for the new life lying so vulnerably in her arms. That's nonverbal appreciation taken to its maximum.

When you express your appreciation to another person, let the tone of your voice reflect your warm feelings of gratitude. Allow your appreciation to show in your facial expressions. Look upon the person in a way that expresses how you value him or her. Your appreciation will be that much fuller, and have that much more impact, when you show it with all of your being.

Vibration Can't Be Forced

Appreciating someone is such a wonderful thing, it can be tempting to give it lip-service. What's the harm in saying, "Thank you for always being supportive of me," even if the person is only mildly and infrequently supportive of you?

The harm is that you risk diminishing the power of your appreciative vibration. Appreciation must be genuine in order to have impact. Its vibration can't be forced. If you are not truthfully thinking and feeling appreciation, you will not be emitting its genuine vibration.

Let's say you had dinner and went to a movie with a friend. You enjoyed the food and the conversation, but you didn't like the movie, and were annoyed by your friend's trying to convince you of its merits. If you say, "What a great evening; I really appreciate our time together," you can feel that you're not telling the truth. You feel phony, because only part of that statement is true, and your nonverbal expression of appreciation is likely to be weak. Your friend won't feel especially valued, because the vibration you're emitting isn't genuine appreciation. With vibration, truly, "what you give is what you get."

So don't force yourself to appreciate. Instead, find whatever specific portion of the evening you can appreciate totally. For example, you could say, "What a great conversation we had over dinner; I'm really grateful for how we share ideas and talk about things." Now your appreciation will have a positive impact, for your vibration is one of heartfelt appreciation.

Nothing says you have to appreciate everything about someone! Appreciation works just fine when you're appreciating even something minute about a person or situation, as long as that appreciation is authentic.

Is Your Vibration of Appreciation Coherent?

Once you have added appreciation of others to your repertoire, the three critical aspects of a solid, well-focused vibration of appreciation are in place: appreciation of life, oneself, and others. With your heart and your head—your feelings and thoughts—aligned through appreciation, the power of your vibrational focus is intense. Your vibration is now coherent, and coherence equals power.

Childre and Martin describe coherence in *The HeartMath Solution* as "the logical connectedness, internal order, or harmony among the components of a system." It is a highly desirable state, since it means that everything is working together smoothly and efficiently. Research has demonstrated that when you are deeply feeling appreciation or love, your heart rhythms become harmonious, ordered, and coherent. Your brain waves then harmonize with your heart rhythms, bringing your whole being into a coherent state.

When your whole being is in a coherent state, say Childre and Martin, it's as if you'd switched from the power of a light bulb to the power of a laser. The light particles from a light bulb are diffuse. They are "incoherent" (nonaligned), so the particles go in all directions. In a laser beam, light particles are aligned in a unified or coherent pattern, which results in a focus so intense that, at very high powers, it can cut through steel.

When you achieve a coherent vibration, appreciation is no longer an occasional event for you. The power of your focus is intense. It has become your habitual, normal state of mind, your way of feeling and being. It is the way you go about living your life.

The Power of Appreciation: Intensity

Focusing your vibration of appreciation coherently and intensely allows you to most effectively transform and attract the experiences you desire, as we will describe in detail in chapters 4 and 5.

Transformation and attraction require that you reach the "feeling place" of appreciation—an active, powerful, excited feeling of passion and enthusiasm. To help you find that place, we've developed a focusing and intensity exercise using "biodots" that you can send for (see the back of the book for ordering information). Biodots are small circles made of a liquid crystal that functions as a rapidly acting thermometer.

Traditionally, biodots have been used in biofeedback therapy to help people reduce their stress levels. The biodot monitors blood flow, as reflected by differences in skin temperature. When you are very stressed, for example, your blood leaves your extremities and flows to your vital organs, with the result that your external temperature, such as the temperature of your hands, decreases. When you are extremely relaxed, your blood flows easily throughout your whole body, and the temperature of your hands increases.

When people are learning how to reduce their stress levels using the biodot, they start by recognizing the color of stress. When a person is stressed, the biodot will be black, or in the black-to-brown range (see page 22 for the biodot chart). They are then taught to breathe deeply, and think "hands warm," which shifts blood flow to their hands. The shift in blood flow decreases physiological stress levels, and the person feels better. Successful attempts to reduce stress are evident, because the biodot changes color from black/brown, to green/blue, to purple (with purple reflecting the most relaxed state).

The biodot is also a wonderful tool to help develop your appreciation, and strengthen your ability to generate and maintain an intense focus. When you are in a vigorously appreciative state of mind, valuing and being intensely grateful, the biodot will change from whatever your starting color was, to green or teal. The green or teal color of the biodot represents an "involved" state, where your parasympathetic and sympathetic nervous systems are working together in balance. You are neither tense nor very relaxed. You are actively working your energies in a balanced state between arousal and relaxation, what we think of as exercising your "appreciation muscle."

To use the biodot to help yourself exercise your appreciation muscle, sit in a quiet place, take your telephone off the hook, turn your pager and cell phone off, and make sure you will be undisturbed for about ten minutes. Place the biodot in the dip between your thumb and forefinger, as shown in the following drawing. After a minute or two, the biodot will reflect your "starting color," anywhere from black to green.

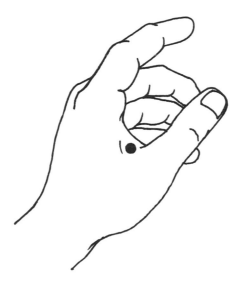

Figure 9.

Your objective is to think thoughts of valuing and gratitude and feel the feelings of appreciation that ensue, until your biodot turns green or teal (regardless of your starting color). Then, you want to keep your biodot at that green or teal level by actively and vigorously thinking and feeling appreciation for three to five minutes.

If you use an egg timer or the like, you won't have to keep looking at a clock. Also, don't stare at your biodot continuously. Since it's often easier to generate thoughts and feelings with your eyes closed, shut your eyes as you appreciate, and open them from time to time only to check on the color of your biodot.

If you find your biodot changing to or approaching a purple color, it means that you're relaxing into a more mellow, receptive mode rather than actively working on thoughts of appreciation. Practice getting into an involved appreciative state, instead of just riding on the good feeling that appreciation gives you— work to actively generate thoughts of appreciation. When you do, your biodot should go back to green or teal.

That being said, everybody's different. If you feel that you are actively, intensely generating thoughts and feelings of appreciation and yet your dot is staying in the orange range or moving into the purple range, don't worry about it. The important thing isn't the color of the biodot, it's learning how your body feels when you are generating intense thoughts and feelings of appreciation, so that you can eventually generate those at will.

Appreciating at this level of intensity takes a fair amount of energy, and five minutes may feel like a long time. It's perfectly fine to build up to the five minutes—for example, by starting with just one minute the first day, going for two minutes the second and third days, and eventually sustaining a vigorous level of appreciation for the full five minutes. You may find that it takes a lot of appreciative thoughts to fill up an intense five minutes!

This is where already knowing what you appreciate about yourself and your life comes in handy. Valuing and being grateful for yourself builds your self-esteem and confidence as you practice using and strengthening your appreciative muscle.

If you spend just one five-minute period a day appreciating with energy and intensity, every day for a month, you will be astounded at the change in your ability to generate and sustain a powerful vibration of appreciation. Once you get the hang of it, you'll be able to generate a strong, clear vibration of appreciation—from your "feeling place"—without a biodot. You can then use the biodot to check on yourself every so often, or when you want to be really sure you're focusing your vibration as intensely as you want to.

What's Next?

As an appreciator, you have developed an appreciative state of mind as your primary world view. In so doing, you have laid the vibrational groundwork for attracting what you desire into your life. The next chapters will help you do just that.

4

Using Appreciation to Transform Situations and Attract Desired Outcomes

You have now learned methods to develop a strong vibration of appreciation. In the rest of this book, you'll learn how to use the energy of that appreciation to transform a situation, or to attract someone or something that you desire.

It's Not about Manipulation, It's about Vibration

Using appreciation to bring about things or experiences that you want in your life has nothing to do with manipulation or control. You cannot use the energy of appreciation to force anyone or anything to do your bidding. What you can do—and herein lies the magic—is deliberately emit a vibration of appreciation for whatever you desire. Your strong vibration is what makes it possible for those experiences that correspond to that vibration to align with you.

Think of appreciation as a musical tone you deliberately sound and project into the universe. Other frequencies hear the call, and gather to produce a particular resonant chord—your desired outcome.

We call this process "attraction" because, according to the phenomenon of entrainment, the strongest, most intense vibration "attracts" other vibrations to align with it—to come over, if you will, to its side, and transform the original vibration into something greater than it could have been alone.

The clearer your vibration (like a musical tone that has been precisely tuned), the more powerfully it will draw other frequencies to complete your resonant chord; that is, to provide your desired outcome. This attraction and alignment happens at the level of frequencies of vibration—the level at which all objects, beings, and experiences are similarly constructed.

Appreciation Facilitates Cooperation

Appreciation attracts desired outcomes because it facilitates cooperation. When you appreciate someone, for example, that person becomes willing to cooperate with you. This cooperation is essential in bringing about your desired result.

Think of someone who values and genuinely appreciates you. Play out in your mind a time when that person let you know just how valuable you were to him, and how grateful he was for your very existence. How does this memory make you feel? Can you feel your body relaxing? Can you feel how your whole being is receptive to this person who appreciates you?

Next, play out a scene in your mind in which this person asks something of you. How willing are you to cooperate?

Now think of a situation in which you weren't valued, where someone was perhaps angry with you or resentful of you. How does this memory make you feel? Can you feel your body tightening up? Can you feel that you are closed off to this person as he unloads anger or resentment onto you?

Next, play out a scene in your mind where this person asks something of you. How willing are you to cooperate?

Appreciation attracts your desired outcomes by first aligning the energies of cooperation between your own vibrational frequency and that of the thing you want.

The PEAR Experiments

Nowhere is the phenomenon we've just described more apparent than in the experiments that have come out of the Princeton Engineering Anomalies Research (PEAR) Laboratory, founded in 1979 by Dr. Robert G. Jahn, former Dean of the School of Engineering at Princeton University. PEAR is devoted to the "rigorous scientific study of the interaction of human consciousness with sensitive physical devices, systems and processes common to contemporary engineering practice," which seeks "to enable better understanding of the role of consciousness in the establishment of physical reality."

In one of the PEAR experiments, a computer randomly generates an equal number of pluses and minuses. A person sits in front of the computer screen, watching a line representing those pluses and minuses wander around the screen aimlessly.

Larry Dossey, in *Reinventing Medicine*, describes how during these experiments, the person then tries to mentally influence the machine to churn out either more pluses (by thinking "go high") or more minuses (by thinking "go low"). Amazingly enough, if the person thinks in the direction of more pluses, the machine will produce more pluses, and vice versa!

What would have been a random array of pluses and minuses in the control situation becomes, with human intention, a nonrandom array. Dossey's statistics show that there is a less than .02 percent likelihood (2 in 10,000) that these results could be explained by chance.

How is appreciation relevant to the PEAR experiments? PEAR researchers found that those people who were most successful at influencing the computer talked about "becoming one" with it. In fact, the person who influenced the computer the most described "falling in love" with the machine.

Appreciation as we define it—valuing and being grateful for—is one of the key components of loving. When you're in love, you rapturously value your mate, and at the same time you are immensely grateful for his or her existence.

"Becoming one," in terms of vibrational frequency, is equivalent to our concept of "aligning with" or "harmonizing" vibrations. The vibrations of the computer and of the person attempting to influence it align, so that both vibrations work together to produce the "more pluses" or "more minuses" that are desired. In essence, the machine's vibrations must be willing to cooperate with the person's vibrations of desire. This cooperation only comes about when vibrations either align exactly or harmonize.

Given how programmed we are to rely on our five physical senses to inform our reality, it may be hard to grasp that the alignments of vibrational frequencies—even of such intangibles as appreciation—bring physical experiences into being. The bottom line is that energy (which is measured by the frequency of vibration) precedes matter. All things exist as energy before they ever become observable as matter.

Energy interacts with energy freely and constantly. It knows no time or space.

In further experiments, PEAR researchers discovered that it doesn't matter if the person trying to influence the computer is in the same room or across the globe. It doesn't matter if the person thinks about what he or she wants the computer to do when the machine is turned on or not. It doesn't even matter if the computer has been run ahead of time, unobserved, but recorded. People can, by focusing on their desired result, influence the computer to produce pluses or minuses whether in the past, present, or future!

This research has staggering implications: your mind can change events and experiences outside yourself. You can literally change the world around you—and appreciation is the key. Here's how Barbara, an AG member, did just that:

My housemate is basically a good person, but we're very different. I like things to be uplifting, peaceful, and happy. My housemate is just the opposite. She's very negative; everything's always, "Wait 'til the other shoe drops" and "Like that'll ever happen." It was getting so I'd actually hang around work, putting off going home. I told her how I felt, and tried to talk to her about being more positive, but she thought I was nuts: "You're just a Pollyanna, get real!" she'd say. So when I decided to try the appreciating thing with her, I really didn't expect it to work. But I figured, heck, anything's possible.

I started focusing just on what my housemate did that was positive, that I could appreciate. She's very responsible about paying her share of the household expenses on time. I valued and was grateful for that. And she's great about fixing things around the house: she'd tackle leaky faucets and toilets and stuff like that. I could appreciate that, and I told her so. I listened for anything even remotely positive in what she would say, and I'd appreciate that. Everything else I refused to focus on—just ignored it, didn't let it matter.

Then one day, much to my complete surprise, my housemate said she was glad we were housemates, that I was a good person to be around. You could have bowled me over with a feather. Her comments became less judgmental, she actually began to say things like "Things will turn out all right," or "Oh I'm sure they'll give you that raise pretty soon." I was so surprised. I could not believe appreciating actually works. But it does! And the proof is—to me at least—that when I stopped focusing on appreciating her, and let my focus stray to whatever negative thing she might do or say, her positive stuff fell off. I started appreciating her again, and sure enough, she became less negative once again. Amazing. Life around our house has gotten really good. And I appreciate it!

Knowing that appreciation can help bring about desired outcomes in your life is good; knowing how to work with the energy of appreciation to bring about those desired outcomes is even better. In the next chapter we'll describe the five steps to transforming or attracting something that you want into your life.

5

Five Steps to Using Appreciation to Transform or Attract What You Want

The energy of appreciation can bring you whatever you truly desire. In this chapter, we describe the five steps you'll take to transform unwanted situations, or to attract new and positive experiences:

Step One
Choose what you want to transform or attract

Step Two
Determine the feelings behind your desire

Step Three
Weed out conflicting thoughts and beliefs

Step Four
Launch your vibration of appreciation

Step Five
Work your appreciation

Throughout the chapter, we'll use the same example, using appreciation to fulfill a desire about which many people feel uncomfortable: the desire for more money. For many of us, this desire for abundance is fraught with unappreciative thoughts and beliefs, implied in questions such as: Are we worthy or deserving of abundance? Is abundance even possible? Is abundance only for the supersmart, the very talented, or the downright criminal? Is abundance purely a matter of chance? Is it strictly for the nonspiritual? Is it a matter of manipulation? Appreciation hardly seems to fit in anywhere.

We'll show you how appreciation works beautifully, even in this most challenging arena of appreciating your way to more dollars.

Step One: Choose What You Want to Transform or Attract

In this step, you clearly articulate to yourself what it is that you want; you ensure that you truly believe your desire is attainable; and if, on reflection, you don't believe your goal can be reached, you adjust it until it is something on which you can confidently focus your vibration of appreciation.

First, describe what you want to transform or attract. If you desire abundance, "I want lots of money" is a great place to start, but from there, give your desire shape, dimension, and form. Give your mind something more specific to focus on. How do you get specific? Relate your desire to your existing life, as in, "I want to double my current salary," "I want to have five times as many clients/customers as I now have," "I want to increase my sales commissions tenfold," or "I want to be able to easily and comfortably afford all my bills and expenses."

Now you have a desire you can connect to in a real way. This is important, for if your desire has no shape, it will be difficult to launch a genuinely focused vibration of appreciation for it.

Once you've given a shape to what you want, make sure that you believe your desire is attainable. Sit for a moment with your idea of what you want, and ask yourself if you really, truly believe, for example, that you could increase your sales tenfold. Can you see yourself depositing a commission check from a tenfold sales increase? If you can say, "Yes, I totally believe I can increase my sales tenfold. I can believe a check for that amount could be mine, not just once, but on a regular basis," that's great! You'll be able to focus a vibration of appreciation for your desire with clarity and strength. However, while many people wish they could be millionaires, few truly believe that they could receive a million dollars, much less several million. Your desire, therefore, must be both sufficiently specific for you to focus on, and believable to you.

If it isn't, adjust your desire to fit your outlook. If you decide, "Well, I really can't see myself increasing my sales tenfold, but I believe I could triple my sales," that's wonderful. Here is a desire you will be able to genuinely appreciate, so you will then specify your desire in terms of a threefold sales increase.

You can always launch a more ambitious desire later. If you specify what you want such that you are truly aligned with your desire, you are much more likely to attract what you seek. If your desire exceeds what you think is possible, you won't be able to launch a genuine vibration of appreciation, and you will be unable to attract what you want.

Step Two: Determine the Feelings behind Your Desire

In this step, you ask yourself what is the meaning, or value, you place on your desire, and how you feel about it; you then articulate the feelings of gratitude you will experience once you are successful in attracting it into your life.

Feelings are a tremendously important part of appreciating. Appreciation is composed of valuing and gratitude, both of which are loaded with feeling. When you launch your vibration of appreciation for the thing you desire, you want to do so with as much emotion as you can muster. In order to do that, you need to identify your feelings regarding your desire.

Ask yourself what your desire means to you. Only when something has meaning for you do you value it. When your child gives you her first drawing of red and orange crayon scribbles, and proudly declares, "Sun!" you value and treasure that drawing, regardless of its complete lack of monetary worth, because it has meaning for you. It symbolizes your child's wondrous growth and development, her vitality, her delightful existence in your life, as well as the love you have for each other.

Going back to our example, let's say that you specified, "I want to triple my sales commission, to $15,000 per month." Now, what does bringing in $15,000 a month mean to you?

"It means I'm rich!" you yell ecstatically.

OK, now how does that feel?

"It feels great!" you exclaim.

What else does it mean?

"It means..." and here you stop, momentarily stumped. That's normal. Most of us don't articulate what things mean to us, yet it will be difficult to line up a focused, intense vibration of appreciation without a clear understanding of what something means to you.

A good way to determine what your desire means to you is to ask what you could do, be, or have once your desired outcome is realized. How will it change your life? How will it affect those around you? Your work? Your hobbies and other activities?

If you think about it, you may realize that your $15,000 would mean that you could pay all of your bills comfortably every month. You then ask yourself what feelings come along with that: security, relief, comfort.

What else does that $15,000 mean?

Perhaps you could give your child, spouse, or mom those little extras that make life more pleasant. What feelings does that evoke? You smile as you picture the pleasure, the sheer delight of seeing the joy of those you love.

What else?

The money might mean savings—you could finally put something away for that car, boat, or vacation that you want, without having to tighten your belt. How do you feel about that? Excited, you realize. Excited and enthusiastic—and you find that now you want that $15,000 even more!

Anything else?

That $15,000 might finally allow you to contribute to the literacy foundation you've admired for years. What a wonderful feeling that gives you! You feel expansive, fulfilled, happy to be part of making our world a better place. Do you want that $15,000 even more ardently now? You bet.

Gratitude comes on the heels of this valuing. When you realize what your desire means to you, and name the feelings that come with it, it's easy to feel thankful and grateful. You have now generated specific feelings of valuing and gratitude that will go into the overall vibration of appreciation you will launch to attract your desire. Those feelings are clear, focused, and easily felt, because they are based on what's meaningful to you.

Step Three: Weed Out Conflicting Thoughts and Beliefs

Now, ask yourself: "What are my thoughts about this thing that I want? What beliefs do I hold about it, its availability, and my ability to have it? What are the core beliefs I hold that impact my desire?"

For your vibration of appreciation to be most powerful, your thoughts and beliefs must agree with the thing you want. You can't think, for example, "Sure,

I love having money, bring it on!" and expect good things to happen, if in the next moment you look at the lonely dollar in your pocket and think, "What's this? One miserable dollar? What can I buy with you? You're not worth anything." These contradictory thoughts inevitably will result in a contradiction in your vibration.

Contradictory thoughts cancel each other out vibrationally, and nothing happens. In our scenario, as long as you stand there lusting after riches while denigrating what's in your pocket, you're at a stalemate. Instead of a clear, focused vibration of appreciation regarding money, you have a conflicted, muddy vibration, which will not serve to attract the money you seek. You lack the singular focus, the coherence that you need to give your vibration of appreciation maximum power.

This is nothing to worry about. Most of us hold contradictory thoughts and beliefs regarding the things we desire. All you need to do is bring those thoughts and beliefs into your conscious awareness, and work with them—and here's how:

List your thoughts and beliefs regarding money. Beliefs are important to examine, because we often mistake them for fact. But a belief is just a thought or collection of thoughts you've held for a long time. It can be challenged just as any other thought can. You may be surprised at how many of your thoughts and beliefs are negative toward money itself, the goodness of money, or the people who have it.

Examine also your beliefs regarding the availability of the thing you desire. In the abundance example, you would examine whether your first thought is, "There's never enough money." Does money seem to come to everyone but you? Does it leave you almost before it gets to you? Do you fear that if you have money people will steal it from you? Or will you want you to give it to them?

These negative thoughts and beliefs will clutter up your vibration of appreciation about your desire. Change each and every one into something that, at the very least, does not contradict your desire, or, preferably, supports it—as in the examples in the following table.

Current Belief	Changed Belief
Money is the root of all evil.	*Money facilitates many good deeds.*
A dollar isn't worth much of anything.	*One dollar, added to another dollar, added to another dollar, eventually adds up to something!*
I'm always broke.	*Somehow I always manage to get by.*
Taxes will kill you.	*Some people make enough money to pay their taxes and have plenty left over.*
Rich people are heartless.	*Some people are heartless, rich or poor. Many rich people are responsible for hospitals, charitable foundations, scholarships, and all sorts of other heartfelt things.*
When you have money, people take advantage of you.	*Some people will take advantage of you whether you have money or not. Poor people get mugged, too.*
There's never enough.	*Some people have more than enough; I can learn to attract more.*
No matter how much I make, the money just disappears.	*Money sticks to some people; money can stick to me.*

Notice that you're not replacing negative beliefs about money with a utopian ideal of how money should work in your life. "There's never enough" did not become "there's always plenty," because you wouldn't believe that. You may, at some point in time, but for now, "some people have more than enough; I can learn to attract more" is something you can believe. A genuine belief is what will support a genuine vibration of appreciation.

Take a look at your core beliefs, for these can impact your more specific beliefs about your desire. Core beliefs are those beliefs about life that underlie all our other beliefs about more specific matters. Examples are: "Life's a struggle, then you die," "I'm the luckiest person I know," "The only way you get anything in this life is by hard work," or "I'm always in the right place at the right time."

If you hold negative core beliefs, such as "Life's a struggle, then you die," or "The only way you get anything in this life is by hard work," then attached to your vibration of desire for money will be this belief that you have to struggle or work hard, with the obvious consequence—the dollars you desire will come hard to you.

Without a frequency of ease in your vibration of desire, the dollars you desire can't come easily to you. We don't know of anybody who launches a vibration of appreciation for abundance by saying, "I appreciate struggle, so make sure I have to sweat for these dollars"! But that is precisely what may happen if you fail to look at your core beliefs, and change them as needed. As for contradictory thoughts or beliefs about your desire, see the table on the next page for some examples that show how to change core beliefs.

Once you're satisfied that you've explored your thoughts and beliefs thoroughly, make a list of your key money-appreciative thoughts and beliefs. Use this list to create abundance-supporting affirmations (positive statements by which you affirm something in order to give it reality). Repeat these daily to yourself. A list of affirmations that support abundance might look something like this:

- Money is great.
- Money is the root of all sorts of good deeds.
- I can be rich without being a jerk.

Current Belief	Changed Belief
Life's a struggle, then you die.	*Life has its ups and downs, and I'm getting into the ups more and more.*
The only way you get anything in this life is by hard work.	*Some things come by working hard, some by working smart, and some wonderful things just fall out of the clear blue sky.*
It's all about whom you know.	*It's all about how you think, feel, and vibrate.*

- Money can come to me easily and joyously.
- I am a magnet for money.
- My life gets better and better all the time.
- I am always in the right place at the right time.

Repetition gave your present thoughts and beliefs their power; repetition will give your new thoughts and beliefs their power as well. Your new abundance-supporting thoughts and beliefs will become a new vibration, aligning with and attracting experiences that validate them, just as your old abundance-resisting thoughts and beliefs inevitably attracted experiences supporting them.

Like attracts like. As you repeat your list of affirmations daily, you strengthen and solidify the focus of your appreciation.

Step Four: Launch Your Vibration of Appreciation

You've done all the ground work: you've chosen what you want to transform or attract; you've articulated the feelings behind your desire; and you've changed any conflicting thoughts or beliefs. Now it's time to launch your vibration of appreciation.

In this step, you start by valuing and being grateful for what you already have. Then you launch your desire vibrationally with clarity, focus, and intention, all the while replacing any intruding negative thoughts with positive thoughts.

Too often, when we have less of something than we want, we denigrate what we do have. If you think, "My bills are too high," you are expressing dissatisfaction with your current income. You aren't appreciating what the money you now have can do for you; instead, you pay attention only to what it can't do. You are critical of your current condition.

Such an attitude makes it difficult to attract anything different. As long as your vibration around money, for example, is critical, blaming, and dissatisfied, you will align yourself with the vibrations of further money situations about which you will be critical, blaming, and dissatisfied! You cannot attract more dollars if you don't appreciate the dollars you already have. Instead, think, "I am grateful that my current income can pay some of my bills." Now you are aligning with a positive vibration about money. Appreciating the dollars you have, with enthusiasm, will most rapidly bring more dollars to you. If you have but one thin dime to your name, treasure it. If you have a fortune, even as you want more, treasure it. Develop a sense of value and gratitude for the money you have, no matter how little or how much.

"Wait a minute," you say. "If I'm satisfied with this one thin dime, won't I just get stuck with only this one thin dime?" Not if you're launching a vibration of desire for more. Don't confuse the vibration of the specific desire you are launching with the vibration of your general appreciation of money. Appreciating the money you have is the foundation from which you can successfully launch appreciation for the money you desire. It is not the end of the story.

If you have none of the thing you desire, so that you are not simply trying to attract more, but are starting from scratch, it's even more important to have a positive appreciation of that thing. For example, just because you don't have any money, that doesn't prevent you from valuing and being grateful for money in general. So, if you think, "I have no money at all; I'm a good-for-nothing," ignore those thoughts and shift your focus quickly to affirmations such as, "Other people attract money, so can I," and "Money is a wonderful thing; I can feel the deliciousness of it." The affirmations you create will help sustain your positive vibration around your desire.

Once you value and are grateful for what you already have, it's time to launch your desire vibrationally.

In a place where you won't be disturbed or distracted, sit comfortably, and close your eyes. Think about all that you value in the thing that you wish to attract. Think about the good things it will do for you. Think in personal, intimate terms that have true meaning for you.

Using the money example, don't think in general terms, such as "It'll let me travel," but be more personal and specific: "Dollars for that Disney cruise I want to take with my family." Be grateful, with all your heart, for the wonderful things your desire will bring to you. Cherish the good feelings of security or comfort, for example, that "more dollars" holds for you. Be grateful for these good feelings. Focus on appreciating the thing that you desire with great intensity.

Feel your appreciation in this way—alternating between valuing, cherishing, treasuring, and being grateful—with all your might for three to five minutes. Use your biodot to help you, if you wish, and then relax. Let it be done—your vibration of appreciation has been launched, and it will seek to align with that which will fulfill your vibration. Appreciation attracts more things to appreciate.

If you could keep a clear, focused vibration of appreciation as just described, there'd be no more to say—your desire would come winging back to you with surprising speed. However, what frequently happens is that intrusive thoughts and feelings get in the way of launching a clearly focused vibration.

For example, there you are, appreciating away, and in creeps the "what if" syndrome:

"What if this doesn't work?"

"What if nothing happens?"

"What if I'm not doing this right?"

The list is endless. These "what ifs" reflect worry, fear, or doubt, and sometimes all three at once. Worry, fear, and doubt do not mix well with appreciation. It's hard to genuinely value and feel grateful for an experience when you are simultaneously worrying about it, fearful about it, or doubting it. Your vibration becomes discordant, and as such, cannot harmonize with the thing you seek.

If you allow worry, fear, or doubt into your vibration of appreciation, you will create a self-fulfilling prophecy. You won't be able to attract your desire to the degree you want, because your vibration will not be maximally focused. So when worry, fear, or doubt crosses your mind as you're mightily trying to launch your desire, simply say, "I don't need to think about that now," and go right back to valuing and being grateful for the thing you desire.

Later, you can examine those worries, fears, and doubts and work through them, replacing them with positive thoughts that will support your appreciative intention, as in the examples in the table on the next page.

Congratulations! You've launched your desire! Now you're ready to receive it. You do that in the next step, working your appreciation.

Step Five: Work Your Appreciation

Once you've launched your vibration of appreciation for that thing you desire, anticipate its arrival with joy and enthusiasm, and constantly look for signs of its

Worry, Fear, or Doubt	More Positive Thought
What if this doesn't work? Then I'll be back to square one.	*If it doesn't work, I can go through the steps again. I'll be better at it from having done it before.*
What if I attract the wrong thing?	*I'm launching a very specific vibration, and I know that like attracts like.*
What if I'm lousy at vibration and can't attract anything?	*I can work on valuing and being grateful more, and I can focus and intensify my vibration of appreciation so that I attract what I want.*
What if I'm not intense enough?	*I'll be able to generate more intensity as I practice.*
What if what I want doesn't want me?	*Vibration aligns with like vibration. As long as I'm launching a desire that's within the scope of my belief, there's no reason why my vibration of appreciation shouldn't attract it to me.*
What if I'm not doing this right?	*It's OK if I don't do this perfectly; I'll do it well enough and I'll get better as I do it more.*

coming into your life. In our example of attracting abundance, this does not mean to look for $15,000 under your pillow tonight. Nor does it mean that your boss will walk in tomorrow morning, beaming, as he announces that he will triple your salary.

What it does mean is that your vibration of appreciation will begin to attract experiences, situations, and people that align in some way or another with the thing you seek. Your job is to "work" your appreciation: to be alert to the unfolding of your desire, to take appropriate actions to further it, to be open to the sometimes surprising vibrations you'll attract, and to consciously choose attitudes and feelings that support your desire.

For example, the vibration of your "triple sales" will begin to align with experiences you have; you may overhear a conversation that gives you an idea about how to attract more customers, or you may see a billboard that reminds you about a promotion you could offer to one of your customers, or your boss may give you a customer everyone else has found too difficult to handle.

Here's where you start "working" your appreciation. Whenever something comes along that is even remotely connected to the fulfillment of your desire, appreciate it, value it, and be grateful. Be on the lookout for such events, and act on them.

For instance, when you overhear a conversation that gives you an idea about how to attract more customers, don't just file it under "good ideas." Be aware that this idea may be a path toward your $15,000 desire. Act on it.

When the billboard reminds you about that promotion you could offer a customer, pick up the phone, call the customer, and offer it.

And when your boss says, "Here's Mr. Smith. No one else can deal with him; it's your turn," don't think, "Great, just my luck, another impossible-to-please never-spend-a-dime customer." Instead, appreciate the opportunity: "I might just be able to turn old Scrooge around—who knows? It's worth a try."

So be alert to the infinite number of ways vibration will start aligning with your desire. Value the ideas and opportunities that come your way, be grateful for them, and *act on them.*

Appreciation does not stop once your vibration of appreciation has been launched. Appreciation is both your intention and your initial action as you vigorously launch your vibration of appreciation. But that is not all there is to it.

Think of your desire as unfolding in a series of events leading to its eventual fulfillment. As early opportunities come along, you are receiving the budding results of your vibration of desire. It is vital that you act on these opportunities. Action makes things real. Use your common sense and best judgment to determine whether or not an opportunity is appropriate to act on, as not every opportunity will be. But just be sure that you do, at some point, take action.

When you launch your vibration of appreciation for your desire, be open for the vibrations to align in any number of ways. Be receptive to surprises and unexpected events. The more willing you are for your vibration to align with many different possible vibrations, the more easily your vibration can harmonize with the thing you desire and the more readily you can attract what you want into your life.

You, of course, have the final choice in the way you allow your desire to be fulfilled, and it's important that you exercise it. If Mr. Smith maintains his reputation of out-Scrooging Scrooge despite your best efforts, then clearly he's not a vibrational match. Walk away. If you slip and fall in a supermarket because you weren't paying attention to where you were going, and someone says, "Hey, the floor was wet, sue the supermarket and you're sure to get a quick $15,000," walk away. In other words, your vibration of appreciation will align with many vibrations you can choose from. It's up to you to value, be grateful, and act on those vibrations that fit with your core beliefs.

Staying open to the myriad of ways vibration may align with your desire, and working your appreciation, often yield unexpected results. For example, your appreciation for the opportunity to turn Mr. Smith around may impress your boss so much (despite your lack of success) that he promotes you or gives you a truly worthwhile client. Walking away from the "sue-the-supermarket" scenario may be witnessed by someone who values your honesty and offers you a job with more dollars attached. Vibration has all sorts of quirky and surprising ways of lining up with your desires.

Some of those surprising opportunites may at first look like tragedies. For example, a few days after you launch your vibration of appreciation for tripling your income, you may lose your job. "Yikes!" you exclaim. "This isn't what I wanted." Yet, it may be that nowhere in the vibration of your current job could a vibration of "triple sales" link up. As you're working your appreciation, you might have a moment of shock and maybe even panic, but don't despair. In this case, you would take action while appreciating the opportunity to clean up your resume, acquire a new skill, brush up on your strengths, and work on your weaknesses.

With this preparation, you will be sensitive to whatever possibilities may present themselves, no matter how small or seemingly unrelated to your desire. In days ahead your vibration of appreciation for triple sales will align with a situation or person who will help in the unfolding of that desire. Your job is to keep appreciating what comes, and keep moving forward.

Work your appreciation with your attitude as well. Expect your desire to be fulfilled, and be willing to exercise patience. Don't test the vibration of abundance by asking every five minutes, "Is the money here yet?" Just as a child's "Are we there yet?" doesn't get him to his destination any faster, "Is it here yet?" doesn't help.

Adopt an attitude of trust. You've launched your focused vibration, now trust that vibration can do nothing other than hook up with a like vibration. It's scientific! Keep yourself on course by cherishing your desire regularly, always with great appreciation, and appreciating whatever you currently have.

By continually valuing and expressing gratitude for whatever comes your way, while expecting the fulfillment of your desire, the strength of your vibration of appreciation increases, and the thing you seek can come to you all the more easily and rapidly.

You are in an emotional state of happy expectation, because all along the way you are perceiving the small and large ways in which the fulfillment of what you want is developing.

Eagerly anticipating or happily expecting the thing you desire is important. It keeps you from falling into a state of longing—that is, thinking about how unhappy you are that you don't have the thing you want. Longing conflicts with appreciation. Try longing for something at the same time as you value and are grateful for it. You'll find it's nearly impossible to do. Choose to *appreciate* the thing you desire rather than long for it, and you're much more likely to attract it.

That's all there is to it. Five easy steps to follow to experience the magic that appreciation can be. The steps outlined on the following page provide you with an easy-to-follow guide that you can keep handy for ready reference. Apply these steps to whatever concerns you, whether it is getting your mother-in-law to treat you with respect, improving your health, transforming your love life, or attracting a fulfilling career.

In subsequent chapters, we'll help you get started applying the five steps of the power of appreciation to specific circumstances involving relationships and work.

The Five Steps to the Power of Appreciation

Step One: **Choose What You Want to Transform or Attract**
- Give shape to what you want. Be specific.
- Make sure your desire is within what you believe is possible.
- Make adjustments, if necessary, until that's so.

Step Two: **Determine the Feelings behind Your Desire**

- Figure out what your desire means to you; ask yourself what its value is to you.
- Explore your feelings relative to your desire.
- Generate specific feelings of valuing and gratitude.

Step Three: **Weed Out Conflicting Thoughts and Beliefs**

- Explore your thoughts about the thing you want.
- Examine your beliefs about it, its availability, and your ability to have it.
- Replace negative or obstructive beliefs with positive ones.
- Examine and change any negative core beliefs.
- Work with affirmations supporting your new beliefs.

Step Four: **Launch Your Vibration of Appreciation**

- Appreciate what you already have.
- Launch your desire with focused, intense appreciation.
- Clear out any worry, fear, or doubt that gets in the way.

Step Five: **Work Your Appreciation**

- Be alert to the unfolding of your desire.
- Take action.
- Be open to the variety of ways in which vibration aligns with what you want.
- Adopt an attitude of trust, and hopeful, enthusiastic expectation.

6

Appreciate Your Way to Loving Relationships

Whether the important relationships in your life revolve around a spouse, partner, friends, or family, these intimate relationships often contribute the most—or the least—joy to your life. Appreciation can make an amazing difference in the happiness you experience in your relationships. Although this chapter focuses on transforming or attracting a relationship with a partner, the concepts and skills described apply to all close relationships.

In the Beginning

No one ever gets married saying, "And in five years we'll hate each other and get divorced."

No one ever begins a significant relationship of any kind saying:

"In three years I'll be miserable."

"In six months I'll look at this person and wonder 'What was I thinking? We have nothing in common.'"

"In eighteen months I'll be bored out of my mind."

"In two years I'll cringe at the sound of this person's voice."

"In four years I'll be the victim of abuse."

"In seven years I'll beat this person to death."

No one says any of these things. When people first find themselves in love and committing to a relationship, they say, in effect, "I've found heaven with this person, and we'll be happy together forever."

What happens? Why do initially wonderful relationships go sour? Are we all stupid? Naive? Misguided?

No. We've simply stopped appreciating.

Appreciation Goes Hand in Hand with Falling in Love

When you first fall in love, appreciating the beloved Other is as natural as breathing. You are enraptured by everything your sweetheart says or does. You are on a fascinating journey of discovery, as you see more and more about that person to cherish. You value every moment together. You treasure every word from your beloved's lips. You cherish the late-night phone calls, the surprise e-mails, the way your beloved looks, looks at you, looks at the world. For all of this, and much more, you are immensely grateful.

You are thankful for the day your mate was born, and for the day he or she came into your life. You are amazed and delighted at how your whole life has changed. Life was dull and without luster before your mate's arrival; since then, life sparkles and glitters. You thank your lucky stars. You view and review the moments of your first meeting, profoundly grateful for that time and all the time spent together since. You are in a state of constant, intense, and all-encompassing appreciation.

Fast-forward two years. You hardly look up when your mate walks in the door. You say a cursory "Hi, how was your day?" and go right back to what you were doing. You vaguely hear your mate telling you about his or her day but don't pay any attention to it until your mate says, "What's for dinner?"

You mutter, "Can't you do anything yourself?" under your breath, and, "Whatever you want, dear," out loud.

"I guess that means take-out again," your mate says, slamming the door to the bedroom.

You sigh and think, "Ah, the joys of marriage."

Without Appreciation, Love Dies

There isn't an ounce of appreciation in the preceding scenario. Not a hint of valuing, not a whisper of gratitude. Without the constant flow of appreciation, love dies. Without appreciation, love suffers an erosion of feeling until eventually nothing is left but the habit of being together.

It's a crying shame, and the cry that erupts loudest when a relationship loses its love is, "You don't care about me anymore!" Right behind it is the cry, "You don't care about the relationship!"

The shame is that more often than not, the person protesting doesn't care about the mate or the relationship either. Not caring means that you don't value your mate or the relationship as you once did, and you are not grateful for his or her existence in your life.

Feeling that your mate no longer cares about you or the relationship means that you no longer feel valued, nor do you feel his or her gratitude for your existence. A sorry state of affairs, and a truly unnecessary one.

Appreciation Gets Love Going Again

Fortunately, appreciation is one of the easiest energies to revive. You start simply by choosing to think appreciative thoughts instead of critical or negative ones. As you change your thoughts about your mate and your relationship, your feelings will follow. Once appreciation is at work in a relationship, the love starts to flow again.

Erin, an AG member, describes what happened to her: "I never used to pay much attention to whether I valued my husband or not. I was more into what he was doing that annoyed me. It got to where I was more grateful to the paper boy than I was to my own husband. But now? Even if I see him out the window or talking on the phone, I look at him and think just how much I appreciate him. And I can guarantee it's going to be a wonderful night when I do."

With few exceptions, appreciation alone will revitalize a waning love. Of course, other tools and techniques are invaluable, such as good communication skills, learning how to better negotiate and share, actively seeking to please the other, and being reliable, trustworthy, supportive, and sensitive.

Appreciation, however, feeds and activates the willingness to use these other tools effectively and successfully. Appreciation is the bedrock upon which a thriving and happy love relationship can be built.

So, what happens between that blissful state of initial appreciation and the bored or sarcastic, "Whatever you say, dear"?

What Kills Love:
Criticism, Contempt, Defensiveness, Stonewalling

Dr. John Gottman, a psychologist at the University of Washington, has examined couples' behavior for more than twenty years. In *Why Marriages Succeed or Fail*, he charts with amazing precision the dynamics of a marriage, including what goes wrong and what goes right.

Dr. Gottman identifies the four ways that partners sabotage their ability to communicate effectively as "The Four Horsemen of the Apocalypse." These four ways inexorably lead to misery.

The Four Horseman are, from least to most dangerous: criticism, contempt, defensiveness, and stonewalling. As these behaviors become more prevalent, good feelings are pushed aside, and it becomes more and more difficult for the partners to relate to what's good in the relationship, or in each other. Left unchecked, criticism and contempt will lead to defensiveness and stonewalling. He likens the insults used in contempt to assault weapons, and says that contempt is "perhaps the most corrosive force in marriage."

Appreciation: The Antidote to Criticism and Contempt

Dr. Gottman's remedy for criticism and contempt is love and respect. Appreciation is love and respect made practical. As a potent antidote to criticism and contempt, appreciation can transform a hurtful, hurting relationship into a loving one. And it can nurture a budding love relationship through the normal growing pains of conflict and disagreement into its joyous fulfillment, without ever going down the path of criticism or contempt.

So where do you start? How do you work appreciation so that it can be magic for your relationship?

Appreciate Your Partner

People often think that a good relationship must be the result of finding "the right person," but that is only part of the story. Any number of people can be "the right person" for you; barring gross incompatibilities, a relationship's happiness is less dependent on the individual person, than on how you view him or her.

For example, when you first fall in love, you may be delighted by your partner's mellow, easygoing approach to life, which nicely balances out your wired, get-it-done-now approach. Six months down the line, however, when something isn't happening the way you want it to, his mellowness is redefined as laziness.

Your partner hasn't changed, but how you view him has. Similarly, your decisiveness was something your partner admired in you, until it meant that you expected him to do something he wasn't in the mood to do (mellow soul that he is), whereupon your decisiveness becomes "controlling" and you become "bitchy." You haven't changed either, but your partner's perception of you has.

Perceptions are also affected by how you feel in the moment. When you feel wronged, upset, or hurt by your partner, you are likely to forget what endears him or her to you, and focus only on what displeases you.

For example, you may ignore how loving your partner is with the kids and focus only on what a slob he is. Both are true. Your partner may ignore how well you handle the family finances, and focus only on how you disdain the sports he loves. Both are true.

But when you focus on what you don't like, don't value, or don't cherish about your partner, you feel resentment. Conversely, when you focus on what you do like, do value, and do cherish, you feel love. The love or lack of it all stems from what you choose to make significant.

When you feel insecure, irritated with your partner, upset, or worried, you're quick to jump to a negative interpretation. For example, you interpret his not picking up his socks to mean that he takes you for granted. When you throw out the last of the cold pizza, he interprets this to mean that you think he's a slob for enjoying cold pizza.

How you feel about anything your mate does or doesn't do comes from your interpretation of the behavior, not from the behavior itself.

Each of us defines behaviors as caring or not caring, and respectful or not respectful. Often, however, your partner may not define a behavior the same way that you do. If your partner doesn't say "I love you" as he leaves the house, you may define this to mean, "He doesn't care for me as much anymore." Your partner may define it as "I was in a hurry and had other things on my mind." When your partner calls you "the little woman" in front of a coworker, you may define this as a mark of disrespect. Your partner may define it as a term of endearment.

Much of the time, we don't talk to our partner about what meaning he or she assigns to any given action. Even when we do, we may then fight about it. For example, if your partner says he didn't say "I love you" because he was in a hurry and had other things on his mind, you may retort, "Well I don't think you really care about me, if you have too much on your mind to remember to say 'I love you.'"

Dr. Aaron T. Beck, founder of cognitive therapy, has worked with hundreds of couples, and notes in his book, *Love Is Never Enough*, that as a partner defines one behavior as indicating lack of caring or respect, he or she begins to notice another behavior that fits this definition, and then another. It snowballs. Eventually, cherished qualities (such as sensitivity, consideration, and responsiveness) undergo what Dr. Beck calls the "Grand Reversal," in which they are replaced with their polar opposites (in this case, insensitivity, inconsiderateness, and nonresponsiveness). The impact on the relationship is devastating.

Appreciation enables you to perceive your partner's behavior in a positive light, to see its value and be grateful for the behavior. When you interpret your partner's words and deeds with a desire to appreciate, you greatly increase the likelihood of loving feelings.

Terry, an AG member, recalls how her whole outlook changed when she stopped interpreting her boyfriend's behaviors and started appreciating them:

When my boyfriend would say, "Gee, thanks for doing the dishes," I would think, "Yeah, right, isn't that what I'm expected to do?" Then I would think, "Alright, maybe he does expect me to do the dishes, but at least he's appreciating it." But he wasn't expecting it—and that was a revelation. He wasn't expecting me to do anything, and then when I did something I got appreciated for it!

The more you appreciate about your partner, the more you will find to appreciate. Practice appreciating your partner when all is going well, so you will have a good stock of things to appreciate that can help you through the rough times. Appreciation is not a guarantee of no rough times. But it does allow you to get through those times more easily, with less hurt or damage, often emerging on the other side with a stronger, richer relationship. As Thomas, an AG member, notes, "I've been pretty good at amplifying the negative. I realize that if I use that power to amplify the positive, I can just turn it around and be powerful in the other direction." This kind of power is what makes relationships grow stronger.

List Your Appreciation

Write down all the things you value about your mate—big or small, significant or ridiculous. If you cherish the way he carefully dries his toes, one by one, write it down, right next to how he can always make you laugh. This list is for you, no one else. Take several days to compile your list, adding to it whenever you discover something else to cherish and be grateful for about your mate. Actively look for more to appreciate, for the more you appreciate him, the more loving feelings will emerge.

Then write down all the things you don't like or value about your mate. Then, for each item on this list, find something to appreciate. For example, if you don't like his love of sports, you could appreciate the fact that sports make him happy. Write this down. You can appreciate his dedication to his favorite team, for it is like his devotion to you. You can appreciate how spirited and alive sports make him feel. You can appreciate the conversation it affords him with his buddies. All of these make it possible for you to clear out of your vibration your negative thought, "I don't like his love of sports." Without this negative thought, your appreciation vibration is stronger, allowing greater love to flow toward your mate.

This takes practice! The next time your mate plunks down in front of the TV to enjoy yet another football game, instead of thinking, "Not football again!" which will sour your interaction, stop yourself, and deliberately bring to mind some of your appreciative thoughts about this behavior, such as: "Oh, he's going to be happy—how great!" or "What a devoted guy—always there for his team," or "This will make him popular with the guys."

But be genuine. If "what a devoted guy—always there for his team" is followed by the thought, "but not there for me," then this is not an appreciative thought for you. You have issues about how much attention you receive, which need to be resolved before you can appreciate your mate's attention to sports. If all you can appreciate is the fact that he is at home, at least in body, then start there.

Vibration harmonizes with like vibration and attracts experiences that match it. The more you focus on valuing and being grateful for your mate's behaviors, the more your appreciation of your mate grows, and in turn the more your love grows.

Appreciation Contributes to Good Communication

Good communication is a cornerstone of a successful relationship, and appreciation gives you another way to build that communication.

Your perception of your partner affects your response and behavior toward him. When you are actively appreciating him, you look for the value in his actions and words. This appreciative focus changes how you communicate, because when you're deliberately looking for things to value, you interpret whatever your partner says or does in the best possible light. You give him the benefit of the doubt. You seek clarification, rather than jumping to conclusions, because you're not looking for lack, for failure.

For example, if you're looking for value, wanting to appreciate your mate, when she says, "You look tired," you'll perceive her comment as concern for your health and well-being. You'll say, "Thanks, honey, that's nice of you to notice; yes, I am tired." If, on the other hand, you are not looking to appreciate your mate, you might say; "Gee, thanks; I don't need you to tell me that," perceiving her comment as criticism. It is this sort of interpretation that damages good feelings between partners.

According to Dr. Gottman, there is a consistent ratio of positive to negative statements made by couples. Couples who function well say five positive things to each other for each negative thing. If we take Dr. Gottman's 5:1 ratio as a rule of thumb, then you can see how important it is to make sure you are appreciating your mate a good deal more often than not.

So make appreciating your mate a habit. Then, even if you forget to appreciate your mate occasionally, you will still have plenty of appreciation permeating your relationship.

Balance Appreciation of Yourself and Your Partner

It is important to maintain a balance of appreciating yourself and appreciating your partner. Value your own position, boundaries, and desires, and at the same time value your partner's positions, boundaries, and desires.

Appreciation shouldn't turn you into a "Yes, dear, whatever you say" automaton. It doesn't mean that you always agree with your partner. Balanced appreciation of yourself and your partner means that, in any given circumstance, you take into careful consideration both your partner's and your own valuable self, desires, and preferences. Neither person should be given short shrift.

For example, let's say that you want to set aside money for your child's college fund; your husband wants to save for a new car. Using appreciation to work through your differences, value both desires. Don't elevate one over the other. Appreciate both your concerns and your husband's, and work together toward a solution you will both appreciate. Now you're valuing both yourself and your husband, which ultimately benefits each of you individually, and the relationship as a whole.

Appreciation Puts You in Charge of Your Feelings

Sometimes, in a relationship, you feel like you're a victim of love, always at the mercy of your partner's moods or emotions. If he's being nice, you feel good; if she's being nasty, you feel bad. When this happens, you are emotionally reactive to your partner, instead of maintaining your personal emotional integrity. Appreciation can help you keep your good feelings going regardless of your partner's current emotional state.

If your partner is in a bad mood, for example, appreciate that he is taking care of himself by grumbling, and simply let him go through it. Keep on an even emotional keel by reminding yourself of all that you value about him, about the relationship, and about yourself. Switch your focus to whatever does make you feel good, and appreciate that good feeling so as to strengthen and renew your own vibration of appreciation. Since you are not fueling your partner's bad mood vibrationally by feeling bad because of it, his bad mood vibration can dissipate more readily.

As tempting as it may be to moan and groan and feel sorry for yourself when your mate is being less than his wonderful self, it is vibrational suicide. Your self-pitying complaining will feed into his orneriness, and the vibration thus generated will be all about negativity, inevitably attracting negative results. Defuse the power of your mate's negative vibration by ignoring it, and maintaining your own appreciative stance.

It is not always easy, but it is always rewarding, as Karen, an AG member, noted: "What irritates me is when I'm confronted with a vibration and I'm not stable enough to deal with it compassionately and easily. It's hard to bend and be flexible; I just bounce back in retaliation. Appreciation helps me maintain a completely different focus, and I don't get irritated. It gives me the strength and willingness to hang in there with people long enough for me to appreciate them."

Using appreciation as your primary focus does not mean that you should ignore serious problems. If your partner's version of a bad mood is to wreck furniture, get drunk, or become abusive, appreciation of yourself means that you take immediate charge of your well-being. Leave, if you have to; don't subject yourself to dangerous behavior. Even in these extreme circumstances, you don't have to let your partner's inappropriate behavior dismantle your vibration of appreciation. Instead, focus your appreciation on yourself, your well-being, and the steps you take to care for yourself.

Appreciation Leads to Problem Solving

Differences of opinions and preferences, and outright areas of conflict, are inevitable between two people in a close relationship. Typically, we marshal our arguments according to the stance, "I'm right, you're wrong," and the ones who can stick it out the longest are the ones who get their way.

When you appreciate your mate as well as yourself, conflict is no longer an expression of "I'm right, you're wrong," but instead, "What I want is valuable, and what you want is valuable; we're *both* right." With this mind-set, appreciation supports and facilitates problem solving. You no longer seek to stand on your righteousness. Instead, you actively seek to value both positions, and you open the door to solution-oriented brainstorming that can result in the fulfillment of both your desires.

Beth, an AG member, tells her story:

We were doing OK as a couple, until the kids came along. My husband is real laid back, a mellow kind of guy, and his idea of child rearing was to slap a diaper on the kid, turn him loose, and let him play. Mine was to childproof everything in sight, do Mommy-and-Me classes, and buy armloads of educational toys. Well, this led to terrific arguments. My husband would say I was stressing our child out, I would show him all the studies showing how important it is to give your child a stimulating and structured environment. Neither of us would budge, and the level of constant tension in our home was awful.

When I started learning about appreciation, I thought, "What better area to try this stuff out on?" I couldn't just accept that my husband's ideas were valuable, so I asked him why he thought the way he did. He already knew why I thought the way I did—I'd practically rammed it down his throat. Anyway, I forced myself to listen, to really listen to what he was telling me and try to value his point of view, and finally I realized he had some legitimate ideas. Our child did need do-nothing time as well as educational time, goof-off time as well as structured task-oriented time.

Once I was willing to see value in what my husband thought, I found it easy to be grateful for his input, and he did the same with me. We began to agree on a mix of activities for our children, and I think our kids are better off for it. Of course we still disagree and butt heads (he may be mellow, but he's stubborn!), but we are much quicker now to stop and try to find something to appreciate in each of our positions, so our fights don't last long, and we find a way to handle things together much more easily.

Appreciation Facilitates Cooperation

Appreciation facilitates cooperation. Instead of stubbornly protecting your right to maintain your interests and hobbies, when you appreciate your and your mate's way of doing things, you become willing to find ways to accommodate both preferences. You stop competing against each other for "my way" and look to cooperate together for "our way."

Competition ruins relationships. Struggling against each other leads to bad feelings. When you compete against each other, more often than not, neither of you is satisfied. When you appreciate both your partner's and your own preferences, you seek to fulfill them both. As you work cooperatively toward that end, your individual satisfaction grows. As your personal satisfaction increases, so does appreciation of your ability to work together, and as a couple you become stronger. You both appreciate your relationship.

Wayne, an AG member, talks about his experience:

> It's funny, but now I almost welcome our disagreements, because instead of tearing us apart, like they used to, they've become ways of getting closer, and we actually get more of what each of us wants, individually. So when my wife wanted to go freelance last year, instead of my panicking over losing the security of that second income, with the fear of the added financial burden I was sure it would place on me, I knew we would be able to talk about it.

I knew my wife would appreciate my desire to continue to share our financial responsibilities, and she knew I would do my best to appreciate her wanting to explore new work options for herself. We were both determined to maintain appreciation for each other's desires, as well as appreciation for our relationship.

With that, we were able to figure out that if we trimmed certain expenses, and if my wife negotiated a part-time position with her company, giving her time to get established on her own, we'd be able to satisfy *both* our desires. It felt really good to support her new goals, and know that she supported what was important to me. It sounds simple when you put it that way, but I think if we hadn't been already well-practiced in appreciating ourselves and each other, the experience could have really damaged our relationship. We would have been competing to satisfy our individual desires, rather than understanding, through appreciation, that we could both be satisfied.

Appreciate the Relationship Itself

A relationship is something to appreciate. A relationship allows you to share experiences. It lets you see yourself through someone else's eyes, and if that can be annoying at times, it is also a wonderful opportunity for self-awareness and growth. A relationship provides companionship, affection, entertainment, support, and caring. It allows you to share responsibilities and combine your abilities and assets of all types: mental, physical, emotional, and financial. All of these characteristics can be valued and cherished. Grow the love in your life by appreciating your relationship itself.

For example, value how wonderful it is to wake up and snuggle in someone's sleepy arms in the morning. Cherish how good it feels to lie, still half-asleep, and recount your dream to a willing pair of ears. Value how precious it is to have dinner with someone who cares about you and whether you had a nice day. Appreciate these special things and the many more that your relationship affords you.

Like attracts like. As you increase your vibration of appreciation for your relationship, aspects of the relationship to appreciate will increase.

As you appreciate the relationship itself, you start looking at it differently. The relationship itself acquires more meaning and importance. You become more willing to make the effort to keep it growing. If you find that you hold negative attitudes about marriage or relationship, even jokingly, weed them out—expressions like "the old ball and chain" don't belong in an appreciator's vocabulary. Negative attitudes interfere with the positive vibration of appreciation of your relationship. They devalue it, however subtly, and entrain a vibration of unhappy feelings.

Sometimes negative attitudes are evidenced in what is not spoken. You can fail to appreciate your relationship simply by not saying anything positive, as was commented on by Kim, an AG member: "I think of the woman who's been married twenty years, and asks her husband if he loves her and he says, 'I married you, didn't I?' He hasn't said the words 'I love you' since, but she's supposed to know that she's appreciated because he married her and he's still there." Such an attitude doesn't support or enhance a relationship. Appreciation is at its most powerful when it is expressed overtly, as well as in your heart.

Spend time every day appreciating your relationship. Value some specific aspect of it that has significance for you, and be grateful for it. Put all your heart into your appreciation, even if only for a minute. That intensely focused moment of appreciation, repeated on a regular basis, will wondrously nourish the love in your relationship. The feeling you generate is addictive, as Dan, an AG member, noted: "I find that I am actually grateful for the *opportunity* to appreciate my wife, so it's almost like this double-bubble kind of a thing. And I think that's one of the strongest things I've gotten in our relationship—the opportunity to really appreciate the presence of someone like her."

Appreciating in the Face of Infidelity

But what about the really nasty things that can happen in a relationship? If your spouse is unfaithful, you can't very well say, "I appreciate your infidelity." In no way do you value, nor are you grateful for their breaking their marital promise. You're more likely to value and be grateful if something painful descends upon their head—like the ceiling, or a thunderbolt, or a frying pan at the very least!

But appreciation still has an important part to play. If you wish to stay in the relationship, you can appreciate your mate's infidelity as a wake-up call, or as an opportunity to take a good look at what your marriage lacks, or how both of your needs and desires have changed, or whether your communication is flawed. Dealing with the source of an infidelity may lead to a stronger, happier relationship once the dust settles.

If, on the other hand, infidelity is the final straw in a host of problems you've been unable to deal successfully with, you can appreciate your new resolve to leave the marriage. You can value and be grateful for what you have learned while in this relationship. You can begin to appreciate the good life that you will create for yourself.

In both scenarios, and others like them, appreciation changes how you view an unhappy situation, and how you respond to it. Appreciation helps you steer clear of blame and fault-finding, which get in the way of problem solving. Appreciation helps you avoid the pitfalls of prolonged self-pity or victimhood, which keep you stuck on the problem rather than seeking the solution. Appreciation empowers you to seek out resources that you need to resolve the situation and move on.

Appreciation Is an Antidote to Power Struggles

Power struggles result from a "my way or the highway" mentality. They ensue when one or both partners refuse to value, much less be grateful for, the other's obstinate refusal to see things the partner's way. You want the windows open at night, she wants them shut: the battle for power rages as you open them, she shuts them, you open them, she shuts them, all night long. If you tolerate open confrontation, the battle is waged dramatically, accompanied by yelling and screaming. If you don't tolerate confrontation, the struggle goes on passive-aggressively: you open the window on your way to the bathroom, she closes it as soon as she thinks you're asleep; you open it when you wake up in the night, she senses your movement, waits again for signs of slumber, then shuts it once more. In either scenario, each of you clings tenaciously to "my way."

Appreciation can dissolve the whole issue of power and make it irrelevant. When you value your partner's right to his or her desires, you don't want to squash them, either overtly or covertly. When you value your own rights, you're equally unlikely to allow your partner to squash your desires. When you value both your and your partner's desires, you can say, "I appreciate what you want, as I appreciate what I want. Let's get creative, let's have fun seeing how we can accommodate both of our wishes." There is no longer a power struggle; there is only a problem to be mutually resolved.

Cynthia, an AG member, speaks of the power struggle she and her husband engaged in for years:

> We used to have the "remote" fight every night; you know, who gets to control the remote and therefore which show the other one will be forced to watch. It seems so petty! But there we were, hashing it out every night, with one or the other of us either stomping out of the room or making rude comments throughout the show.

When we decided to try appreciating our way through this, we ran up against an immediate brick wall. I couldn't appreciate the World Wrestling Federation under any circumstances, and home decorating shows were the bane of my husband's existence.

So we decided to start by just appreciating that each of us had different, equally valid preferences. Deep breath. After some squabbling over "equally valid" we were able to accept that concept, and then decided to go for the gold: appreciating our different remote styles. I'm a "hit the remote once to find your show and that's it" type, and my husband is a "remotes were made for endless continual channel surfing" type.

We realized there were actually only a few shows each of us really cared about, so we decided to honor those show times as "surf-free zones." If two shows were on at the same time, we took turns watching our show live, and watching the taped version later. For the rest, we alternated nights as to who held the remote. This ridiculously complicated system turned out to work very well for us.

Mind you, the only thing that makes it work is our fierce determination to appreciate both our own choices and each other's choices—which sometimes is a challenge. I mean when was the last time you tried to watch a Seinfeld rerun chopped up with moments from three other shows—and much less appreciate something about it? What cracks me up, is that after all this, we're both watching TV less and either reading or talking more, and having a lot more fun just enjoying time together. I guess when the power-struggle aspect got taken out of the equation, TV became a lot less important. Who would have thunk it...

Appreciation Short-Circuits Abuse

Another kind of power struggle is, in truth, not a struggle at all, but outright domination. In an abusive relationship, one partner imposes his or her will on the other, and will accept nothing less than total submission. Control and coercion may involve emotional, mental, and physical abuse.

Domination cannot exist where appreciation is the governing principle. If your partner values and is grateful for your very existence, and values and is grateful for the unique individual that you are, he or she cannot seek to control you, for controlling you violates your ability to have your own unique desires, boundaries, and positions.

When you appreciate another person, you cannot and would not want to impose your will on that person. Similarly, when you appreciate yourself—your desires, boundaries, and positions—you cannot accept being dominated, for it violates who you are. When you appreciate yourself, even if you find you have been seduced into a relationship of domination, you will not stay.

Appreciation Counteracts Jealousy and Possessiveness

Less obvious forms of control are jealousy and possessiveness. When you love someone, that person becomes precious and valuable to you. You fear losing him or her, and feel jealous or possessive when that fear is activated. This is a natural consequence of loving, and not a problem.

It *is* a problem, however, when the fear of losing the mate is translated into controlling behavior. For example, you forbid your mate to see so-and-so, or you check up on him; where he has been, with whom, and for how long. Perhaps you go everywhere with your mate lest he catch another's eye. Eventually you achieve the exact opposite of what you hoped for. Far from binding your mate more closely to you, attempting to control him stimulates your mate's desire for freedom. Either he will pine away, depressed at the very core from lack of liberty, or leave to recapture it.

When you appreciate your mate, however, that appreciation increases your partner's desire to be with you. Think of it: when someone values you, sees your true worth, and tells you how much he appreciates your intelligence, individuality, sense of humor, quirky ways, or sweet smile, do you want to leave? Quite the contrary, the more someone makes no effort to chain you, the freer you are to enjoy his appreciation of you, and the more likely you are to want to stick around.

Applying the Five Steps to Relationships

Let's look at two situations: transforming a not-so-good relationship, and attracting a new relationship. You'll see how the five steps to using appreciation can work on relationships of all kinds.

Transforming a Not-So-Good Relationship

You're disgruntled. At first, your mate only had eyes for you, but now it seems he has eyes only for the TV, the computer, and his buddies. You want him to spend more time with you, but nagging, prodding, and muttered threats have had no visible impact. You're close to giving up, but he is a good guy and you do love him, so you're willing to try appreciation.

Step One: Choose What You Want to Transform or Attract

You want your mate to spend more time with you. That's a good beginning. Now ask yourself what that means to you, specifically. Give shape and form to what you want. Does "spending more time with you" mean that you want your mate to cook dinner with you? Spend time in meaningful conversation with you? Take walks with you? Go grocery shopping with you? Play scrabble with you? You may say, "All of the above!" but if you then asked yourself, "Do I believe attracting all that is possible?" you might confess that no, you can't see all of that happening.

Instead of setting yourself up to fail, choose something that you believe is possible. For example, you may feel that meaningful conversation might be a stretch, but that cooking dinner or taking walks together is something you can see happening. You can always attract more later on.

Step Two: Determine the Feelings behind Your Desire

What does your mate spending more time with you mean to you? "It means I'm loved," you may respond. Next question: How do you feel when you are loved? You may feel peaceful, relaxed, happy, secure. What else? How will your mate spending more time with you change your life? How will it affect you?

As you reflect on the differences your desire might make to your life, you determine the value of your mate spending more time with you. You may realize that you'd feel more connected to your mate, and that you'd have more of a "together" feeling than you do now. As you think about the value of your mate's spending time with you, allow feelings of gratitude to arise. Feel how grateful you would be for this gift of time with you.

Step Three: Weed Out Conflicting Thoughts and Beliefs

"Well, that'll never happen," you think. "You can't teach an old dog new tricks, and he's stuck in a rut. He's much too selfish to give up his favorite pastimes just for me." It's true, if you hang on to these beliefs, it won't happen. Your beliefs are in direct contradiction with your desire.

Take some time to uncover your beliefs about your mate spending more time with you. Ask yourself: "Do I really believe that he is capable of or would want to spend more time with me?" Then counter your conflicting beliefs with more positive beliefs, as in the following examples:

Current Belief	Changed Belief
He's stuck in a rut.	*A rut is just a habit, and habits can be changed. He used to have excuses for not working out, but he works out regularly now. That's a habit he changed.*
He's much too selfish to give up his favorite pastimes just for me.	*He used to get himself a cup of coffee and never offer me one, or throw away the paper without asking me if I'd read it. He's changed those habits. So maybe it's not that he's too selfish, maybe he just doesn't have a "good reason" to do anything differently yet.*

As we have noted, when you change your beliefs, you should work your way gently into your new belief. A new belief will do you no good at all if you can't wholeheartedly believe it. "He's always thinking of others first" just wouldn't fly right now. You have too much proof of his selfishness.

Your belief, "You can't teach an old dog new tricks," is a core belief, and as such impacts many more areas of your life than your relationship. Be sure to change this belief as well. For example:

Current Belief	Changed Belief
You can't teach an old dog new tricks.	*Maybe that's not entirely true. My mom is elderly and she learned to go on the Internet last year. And people have career changes in their fifties— I've read about that. So maybe you can teach an old dog some new tricks.*

Solidify your new beliefs with the help of affirmations, positive thoughts that you repeat daily, such as:

- People pick up new habits all the time.
- My husband can learn a new habit; he's done it before, he can do it again.
- Old dogs do learn new tricks.
- Anything is possible.

Step Four: Launch Your Vibration of Appreciation

Start by appreciating what you already have. Appreciate the time your husband does spend with you, even if it's very little. For example, there you both are, brushing your teeth in the bathroom together. Value the companionship of the moment, be grateful for the easy comfort of his presence. Don't allow thoughts of "And this is all I get!" to intrude. Notice all the moments your mate does give you, and appreciate them with all your heart. Consciously, deliberately ignore the time he's spending away from you, and keep your focus strong and steady on appreciating the time with your mate you are currently receiving.

Now you're ready to launch your vibration of appreciation for that "more time" you desire. Go to that quiet place inside yourself, and think about all the wonderful moments the "more time" will bring you. Cherish the good feelings this time will bring you. Be grateful for them. Focus on appreciating the "more time" with as much intensity as possible, for about three to five minutes. Then let go, and relax.

Keep your focus clear and powerful by releasing any thoughts of doubt or worry, such as, "This won't work," or "How's he going to change? I can't see him giving up TV."

Let the vibration sort out how your "more time" will be attracted to you.

Step Five: Work Your Appreciation

Working your appreciation truly is the fun part. Be alert to your desire unfolding. If your husband suddenly calls out to you while he's watching TV and you're in another room, "Hey, Hon, did you see this?" don't ignore him.

Don't think: "Is TV all he can talk about?!" Conversing about something that catches his attention may be the beginning of "more time" spent with you. Watch for these small changes.

It's highly unlikely that your husband will turn to you one day and say, "I'm throwing away the remote, forswearing the Internet, and abandoning my friends. From now on it's just you and me, babe." What is more likely is that in all sorts of ways, big and small, your vibration of appreciation for "more time" will result in more time spent together.

As you go along, continually focusing on appreciating whatever time you spend together, you may find yourself prompted to do or say different things. You may be inspired to say, "It's a beautiful day and I was thinking of exploring that old house down by the river. Want to come?" You may have what seems like an irrational desire to ask your husband to teach you to use that new software he bought. Take action! Follow up on these inspirations. These are ways that vibration is working to align with the vibration of your desire.

Stay hopeful, expectant, and enthusiastic about your appreciation for "more time." Keep your faith high and your appreciation strong. Soon enough, "more time" will be a reality.

The only way this wouldn't work is if your mate has within him truly no appreciation of time spent with you, meaning that there is nothing for your vibration of "more time" to hook up with. If this is the case, then consult an appropriate professional (counselor, therapist, spiritual healer), for you may need to rethink your relationship.

Using Appreciation to Attract a New Relationship

But what if you're not in a relationship? You may yearn for a relationship, and want one with all your heart. But you meet only duds, and those may not even come along very often. Meanwhile, every movie, advertisement, and friend getting married seems to cry out "relationship!" at you. "When will it be my turn?" has become your insistent refrain. How can you use appreciation to attract that oh-so-longed-for relationship into your life?

Step One: Choose What You Want to Transform or Attract

"Tall, dark, and handsome" may be what you say you want, but "tall, dark, and handsome" comes in all sorts of packages, which may or may not be what you want. It can come packaged with manipulation, cunning, and selfishness; or with passion devoted only to mental pursuits (there goes your sex life); or with honesty, devotion, and an abiding concern for the good of others.

Create a description of what you want in a mate. You don't need excruciating detail, but do outline the main points that are important to you. For example, a person's hair color may not matter, but honesty and a sense of humor may be very important.

Next, specify the nature of the relationship you want to attract. Is it a relationship of partners? Or best friends plus passion? Or companionship? Or something entirely different? Choose what works best for you, not what society, your mother, or your friends think is desirable in a mate.

Then take some time to sort out whether your description of "the relationship I want to attract" is something you believe is possible. Do you truly believe that the drop-dead-gorgeous, wildly successful, thirty-five-year-old jet-setting entrepreneur who was just honored for his work saving the whales will fall in love with you, settle down, and raise 2.5 children with you behind a white picket fence? If your heart cries out a resounding "Yes!" then go for it.

But if, when you think on it, you admit that a better fit would really be a mellow guy, good-looking in his own way, who works hard and cares enough about his family to bring home a good paycheck, and cares enough about our planet to volunteer for the community clean-up campaign once a year, well then, that's what you go for.

In attracting with appreciation, what's important is not what you want, so much as believing that what you want is possible. You cannot launch a vibration of appreciation for something you believe is impossible. It just won't work.

Step Two: Determine the Feelings behind Your Desire

What does having this relationship mean to you? What will you value about it? For example, is it sharing your life with someone? Knowing that someone cares deeply for you? Having someone to share the responsibilities of life? Raising children together? Write down some of these "things I will value about our relationship," so that you can refer to them often.

Then ask yourself how you will feel when you're in this relationship. Comfortable? Secure? Adored? Happy? Joyous? Peaceful? Excited? As you dwell on all that you will value about this relationship and the feelings you will enjoy within it, allow gratitude to fill your soul. Smile on it, let your whole being fill with thankfulness. Steep yourself in these feelings, for they are what you will use to launch your vibration of appreciation to attract your wonderful relationship.

Step Three: Weed Out Conflicting Thoughts and Beliefs

Our culture is loaded with unappreciative and negative beliefs about men, women, and relationships. Negative core beliefs like the following must be changed if you are to attract the quality of relationship you truly desire. Here are some ideas on how to do that:

Current Belief	Changed Belief
All the good ones are taken.	*Some of the good ones are taken, that's for sure. But I only need one man or woman, and there are billions of people on the planet, millions just in my neck of the woods. I'm sure there are a few good ones out there.*
Men are only interested in one thing.	*Yes, men like sex, but I know my male friends have other interests. If they do, why wouldn't the man I attract have other interests too?*
Women are just out for your money.	*I've been burned, and the divorce cost me plenty, but if I look around at some of my friend's wives, they're not all greedy.*

Current Belief	Changed Belief
Men never want to commit.	*Everywhere I look, it seems men are bolting from relationships, and my last boyfriend got cold feet as soon as it got serious. But there do seem to be some people who are long-term marrieds, and somehow those guys got over the hump of commitment, so maybe I can attract one like that.*
Women are out to change you.	*I remember that girlfriend I had in college; she wasn't like that. And I notice my friend Stan's wife doesn't do it, and they've been together a long time. Maybe I can attract a woman who isn't bent on changing me.*
Marriage spells the end of freedom.	*Well, it certainly means I'd have to be accountable for my time, whereabouts, and who I see. That might not be so bad, actually. I wouldn't mind someone caring about where I am and who I see. Maybe we could talk about how much personal freedom is OK in a relationship—maybe I can attract someone who's open to that kind of discussion.*
It's the old ball-and-chain.	*You know, I don't really believe that. If I look at my past relationships, they may not have worked out, but I never really felt the person was a drag on me.*

Be sure to examine your negative beliefs about yourself as well. For example, you may feel that you are too old or too young, too fat or too skinny, too poor or too rich, too bright or not bright enough, too whatever, to attract the relationship you want. The easiest way to change these beliefs is simply to look objectively at the world around you. Upon close observation, you will notice that happy, thriving, love-filled relationships exist among people of all shapes, sizes, ethnicities, sexual preferences, religions, intellectual abilities, financial situations, states of health, and so on. Love truly finds a way. Dispel your negative beliefs so that you can develop a clear, focused vibration of appreciation to attract the relationship of your dreams.

Create affirmations for yourself to support your new beliefs, such as:

- There's someone for everyone.
- Somewhere out there, there's the perfect mate for me.
- I'm good enough in every way to attract the mate and relationship that I want.

Step Four: Launch Your Vibration of Appreciation

Start, as always, by appreciating your current situation. Switch your focus away from how miserable you feel because you don't have a mate, to appreciating the relationships you currently have with family, friends, coworkers, or pets. Value the companionship in your relationships. Appreciate the fun of sharing your experiences, thoughts, and feelings with the people already in your life. Look deliberately for where you already experience pieces of what you want.

Notice how you respond to people who are in the type of relationship you seek. How do you feel about other couples? When you see a couple kissing at the movies, do you feel jealous? Do you rage inside at the injustice that it isn't you? Do you hate seeing your married or coupled friends, because you feel horribly out of place still being single? It's very hard to have a vibration of appreciation of relationship when you resent all others who are in relationship.

Start looking at couples with a new eye. Appreciate by saying, "Soon that'll be me." Deliberately cultivate an attitude of eager anticipation about your future relationship, letting every piece of evidence of that type of relationship already existing out there in the world be proof to you that "Relationships exist! And mine is on its way"—and appreciate that as much as you can.

Go within to your quiet place. Summon up the wonderful thoughts and feelings about your desired relationship that you developed in step two. Think about all that you will value in this relationship, and let your heart and soul fill with gratitude for the wonder of it. Let your vibration of appreciation grow in intensity until it feels strong and solid, stay with that intense focus for three to five minutes, and then relax. It is done.

Keep your focus of appreciation alive every day. This may at times be difficult, for there is a particular challenge in using appreciation to attract a relationship, and that is the very natural feeling of longing. It is only human to long for your mate to show up, to stare longingly at loving couples, thinking, "When, oh when, will my turn come?" Unfortunately, longing produces a frequency of vibration completely at odds with the vibration of actually having the relationship. Longing has nothing in common with contentment or joy. It is imperative to transform your feelings of longing into feelings that harmonize with a vibration of appreciation for what will be—the relationship you so ardently desire.

This need to release the feeling of longing explains the experience of many people who say, "Just when I thought I'd never meet anyone and had given up on the whole relationship thing—there he was." With the frequency of longing out of their vibration, the vibration of appreciation of a relationship was clear and could now align with the vibration of the experience of a relationship to appreciate.

How, without abandoning your desire for a relationship, do you set aside longing? By choosing to think about what you value in the relationships currently in your life, rather than focusing on the lack of a specific type of relationship in your life.

Step Five: Work Your Appreciation

Even as you steadily flood your current relationships with appreciation, be aware of a new relationship coming into your life. Be open to any number of wondrous and apparently magical ways that your vibration of appreciation will attract your relationship to you. For example, you may be inspired to go to one event rather than another, and you may find yourself wanting to speak to someone you've never noticed before. Don't look for the obvious. Rarely does someone come up and say, "Hi, I'm the relationship you've been looking for."

A more likely scenario: You may feel inspired to join a book club. After a few meetings, you comment to an elderly couple in the club how nice you think it is to see a long-term couple happily married; in the course of conversation, they mention that their son is coming into town the next week and ask if you would like to come to dinner.

You accept, and their son is a total nerd, but the friend he brought with him is amazing, and voila! You're off and running, well on your way to that relationship.

Or, an old friend seems different to you somehow, and what had been platonic friendship blossoms into love. Or your dog poops on someone's lawn with a big "Curb your dog please!" sign on it; as you're trying unobtrusively to get rid of the incriminating evidence, Ms. Wonderful passes by, walking her dog, and clucks in commiseration, and there you go, your new relationship in the offing.

If your new relationship doesn't come along as speedily as you had hoped, review your beliefs about relationships. That's often where vibration gets cluttered up. The power of vibration to link up with like vibration is scientific. Be vigilant in clearing out contradictory beliefs or feelings. Keep looking for things to appreciate about relationships in general, about the relationships you observe, and about relationships you currently have. In time you will attract the relationship that lives so beautifully in your heart!

Heaven on Earth

Love, of course, is what underlies a relationship, but love is not enough. Appreciation, although it is not the answer to everything in relationships, can create many of the conditions that lead to healthy, happy relationships. Actively appreciating the other is the foundation of a thriving relationship; it can transform the *feeling* of love into the *doing* of love; it can turn words of love into the living of love.

And when you put together the feeling of love with the living of love, you truly have Heaven on Earth.

7

Appreciate Your Way 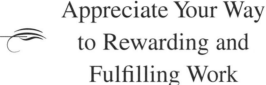 to Rewarding and Fulfilling Work

Work. Something most of us do five days a week, fifty weeks a year, for roughly fifty years.

Work. A tremendously important part of life. Whether you're a homemaker, a dental assistant, a small-business owner, or a CEO, your work impacts how you feel about yourself and your place in the world; how you perceive your value to yourself, your family, and your society; and, more often than not, what determines your success and abundance.

Work. What does that word conjure up for you? Eager involvement in a vocation you love? A duty you must fulfill? A paycheck at the end of the week? Great coworkers you enjoy working with? An obligation you wish you could avoid? A way to pass the time? Something that gets you out of the house? A place to meet people? Situations that challenge your mind? Too much responsibility for too little pay? Endless boredom interspersed with annoyance and frustration? Constant deadlines that stress you out? A hindrance to time spent with your family? Arguments with coworkers? A rude, insensitive, and demanding boss?

For too many of us, work is a hardship, a constant struggle, a sentence we serve until we can retire and finally enjoy life.

Appreciation can change that negative outlook.

When you look at your work through the lens of appreciation, work acquires an ease or flow, and you become focused on a common intention with your coworkers, bosses, and customers. Appreciation helps you recognize your value, your contribution to the larger scheme of things. With it, work ceases to be drudgery and instead supports and enhances your life. Work brings you joy, and in the process, brings joy to others.

Daniel Goleman, in *Emotional Intelligence*, writes of the uplifting effect one man's appreciation for his work had on countless strangers:

It was an unbearably steamy August afternoon in New York City, the kind of sweaty day that makes people sullen with discomfort. I was heading back to a hotel, and as I stepped onto a bus up Madison Avenue I was startled by the driver, a middle-aged black man with an enthusiastic smile, who welcomed me with a friendly, "Hi! How you doing?" as I got on, a greeting he proffered to everyone else who entered as the bus wormed through the thick midtown traffic. Each passenger was as startled as I, and, locked into the morose mood of the day, few returned his greeting.

But as the bus crawled uptown through the gridlock, a slow, rather magical transformation occurred. The driver gave a running monologue for our benefit, a lively commentary on the passing scene around us: there was a terrific sale at that store, a wonderful exhibit at this museum, did you hear about the new movie that just opened at that cinema down the block? His delight in the rich possibilities the city offered was infectious. By the time people got off the bus, each in turn had shaken off the sullen shell they had entered with, and when the driver shouted out a "So long, have a great day!" each gave a smiling response.

Appreciation Helps You Stand Proud

When you recognize and appreciate your role at work, you can see its meaning and significance. Questions of status become less important, since everyone's work has value. You no longer envy others' jobs or salaries. In the absence of comparison, your self-esteem increases. Since you appreciate where you are right now, you are in the best place from which to launch something yet more wonderful.

You give willingly and generously of yourself because you appreciate what you have to offer. Appreciating yourself makes it much easier to appreciate others' contributions. The idea of teamwork becomes a genuine heartfelt reality.

With this perspective, you take responsibility for how you feel at work. You don't wait for someone else to appreciate what you are doing. Instead, you set your own standards, and appreciate yourself every inch of the way. You deliberately look around yourself with eyes of appreciation, and find much to value in your work situation.

Even if your current work is not what you would ultimately like to do, appreciation lets you see how it is benefiting you, as Jason, an AG member, found: "When I graduated from college last year I interviewed for investment banking jobs, but instead ended up selling insurance, which I hated. But now I'm realizing why I'm at this job. Selling makes me show up 100 percent with what I have to offer right away. I can't hang back. I've needed to master this all my life , and I'll bet when I do, the investment banking field will open up to me."

Sometimes you may find yourself in situations in which everybody is complaining and finding fault. Their negative outlook is irrelevant; as you give off a vibration of appreciation, regardless of others' attitudes, your vibration will seek out a like vibration. It must boomerang back to you, for that is the nature of vibration. You will find yourself being appreciated, one way or another. Harold, an AG member, found that the boomerang of appreciation didn't take long to return to him:

I've started to appreciate my job and that's unexpected. I mean, I've appreciated my job to a point, in the old definition of appreciation: "Yes, I'm really glad to have this job; it's a paycheck." This is different. Now I've been appreciating deliberately for a couple of weeks, and all of a sudden, it's really starting to bring results.

We had this meeting today, a departmental meeting. Everybody was there, sixty people or something. They were talking about company philosophy. I'm a contractor so I'm not really a member of this company. But they were acknowledging my work and I really got how welcomed I am; I hadn't felt that before. Then I had a meeting with my boss and his boss, and they let me know how much they appreciate the work I've been doing. They went out of their way to do that, and then asked if they could change the terms of my employment to bring me more into the company. There's a negotiation to do, but it's mostly the acknowledgment that was significant. So significant. It was at a new level."

How can you work appreciation so that it can transform your work experience?

Appreciate Yourself in Your Work

Start by appreciating yourself. Ask: What do I bring to my work? What skills? What particular talents? What parts of my personality—my humor, my flexibility, my promptness, my alertness, my meticulousness, my perseverance—contribute to my job?

You probably take your unique qualities for granted. Instead, value your skills, talents, and contributions. Be grateful for your abilities. You'll see your self-esteem rise almost immediately, and with it the sense of pride that accompanies genuine ownership of your qualities and abilities. Even something as simple as knowing when to say no is a skill to appreciate, as Anthony, an AG member, noted: "I appreciate that I have good boundaries. I appreciate that I am willing to stand up for myself in a way that doesn't damage others, and say, 'Excuse me, this doesn't work for me.'"

When you appreciate yourself in your work, you no longer sing the martyr's refrain, "Nobody appreciates me, nobody cares about me, what I do doesn't matter to anybody." *You* appreciate yourself, *you* care about yourself! With that attitude, you create a frequency of vibration that attracts more to appreciate about yourself. Inevitably, appreciation will come from many other people in your workplace.

Appreciation does not equal arrogance or an overdeveloped ego. Don't appreciate yourself to the exclusion of others, or put yourself above them. Appreciation stays firmly rooted in the here and now. You value your skills and contributions for what they are, without thought of how much better or worse you are than anyone else.

Appreciate What Your Work Does for You

Although a paycheck may be your first thought when you ask yourself to appreciate what work provides you, work actually contributes a great deal more to your life. It provides the outlet through which you express and exercise your talents, skills, and abilities. When you appreciate how your work allows you to express yourself, work becomes far more than a job; it becomes intrinsically valuable in an intimate and personal way. Work becomes a means of personal fulfillment. Maria, a paralegal and an AG member, notes,

> Before I looked at how to appreciate what my work brought to me, I only thought of it as a good-paying job with a lot of hassles and pressures. Now I appreciate that it's a great place to use my mind. I have a good mind. The stuff the lawyers throw at me makes me really use my mind.
>
> So now when I'm faced with a lot of demands and deadlines, I sort of up the ante for myself. I think, "I really appreciate that I get to use my mind here, so come on mind, here's an opportunity to really show your stuff," and I love that I have a job that asks that of me. It's made the pressure not feel like so much pressure—more like an opportunity to rise to the occasion.

The cheerful New York bus driver knows that his work is much more than helping the passengers get where they need to be; he knows that it provides him with a way to spread happiness and good feelings.

Appreciate the Larger Sense of Purpose Work Gives You

Work gives you a sense of purpose, and your work affects other people. When you appreciate how your work allows you to matter in the world, you see your work with new eyes.

For example, you're not just an engineer who designs commercial air conditioning and heating systems. Appreciation helps you see that you're making environments comfortable and healthy for people who work in the buildings with the systems you design. Your work contributes to the overall well-being of people, helping them be more effective and happier.

As a homemaker, you're not just cleaning house, making meals, and picking up after the kids, you're contributing to the family's health and happiness. You're also contributing to the overall health and happiness of your community and your nation, since healthy and happy individuals make for a more viable society. Your work gives you this opportunity. Appreciating your work places it in a larger, more meaningful context, from which you can draw pride and a deep sense of self-worth—as in the following examples.

Occupation	Larger Purpose
Janitor	*Making environments clean and pleasant for people to work in, so they can be happier and healthier as they work, thereby contributing to the overall success of the company or organization.*
Car dealership manager	*Helping people make choices that will work for them, taking into account their lifestyles, families, and budgets; assuring steady employment to other personnel by wisely managing the dealership; encouraging, supporting, and assisting personnel to do well so that they can grow in their skills and accomplishments.*
Bookkeeper	*Helping individuals and companies keep their financial affairs in order, so that they can budget and spend wisely, which contributes to their success, and minimizes stress.*

Any work can be appreciated in this way: from running a mom-and-pop business to manual labor, from fundraising to waiting tables, from recording a song to data entry. No matter what you do—your work has purpose in the larger scheme of life.

How Appreciating Your Coworkers, Bosses, and Employees Improves Your Life

Nobody works in a vacuum. Most of us work directly with coworkers or employees, and most of us answer to a boss. Too often, we resent those whom we work with, and would be happier without a boss looking over our shoulders. However, people thrive on appreciation. Think of how good you feel when someone says "thank you," and points out why they appreciate you.

The truck drivers carrying tons of debris from the wreckage of the World Trade Center in the weeks after September 11, 2001, were spontaneously and openly appreciated by New Yorkers, who lined their route, applauding and holding up "Thank you" placards as the trucks drove by. The looks on those truck drivers' faces was something to behold: astonishment, pride, and a wonderful look of delight at being appreciated.

When you appreciate others, you become more willing to work in concert with them, and their cooperation comes more easily. They know that you value what they have to offer, just as you value what you yourself have to offer. You know and are grateful for what each of you contributes to your mutual goal. It's easy to work harmoniously together, and everyone involved thrives.

In his book *No Contest*, Alfie Kohn notes that cooperation in the workplace is "a shrewd and highly successful strategy, a pragmatic choice that gets things done ... even more effectively than competition does." Studies have repeatedly backed this up, whether individuals are cooperating in the service of a common goal or working toward their individual goals. Cooperation increases access to resources and stimulates creativity, leading to greater efficiency and success for all involved, and it enhances psychological health and well-being. In a cooperative situation, Kohn notes, there are no losers; everybody wins, which assures a high level of self-esteem and mutual respect.

People are so used to being ignored or criticized, they may be surprised at your overt expressions of appreciation. Some may wonder if you have an ulterior motive. No matter—just keep appreciating people genuinely, and soon, most will come to trust it and enjoy your appreciating.

Sometimes we overlook those who are most easy to appreciate, such as the coworker who is always willing to help out. It's important not to take him for granted. In your heart, and to him, express your appreciation. It can be as specific as, "Thank you for helping me get that project out on time," to a more general, "I appreciate how you're always ready to pitch in and help me out." Just remember to look for things to value, and to give voice to your gratitude.

The list of what you can appreciate is endless. However, you may be surprised at how much thought it takes in the beginning to come up with the words! Most of us don't make a practice of openly appreciating coworkers, so it may take a while before your expressions of appreciation flow naturally. Here are some examples to get you started:

"Thank you for showing me how to fix the copier."

"Thank you for being so prompt; it really helps me out."

"I really like the way you organized the waiting room. Thank you."

"I appreciate the equipment you ordered; it works great."

"Thanks for taking out the coffee cups."

"Thanks for reminding me of that appointment."

Be specific, and be appropriate. Appreciating how someone helped you is appropriate; appreciating someone's outfit, however, may or may not be appropriate:

"I appreciate your professionalism, both in your work as well as your presentation of yourself." (Appropriate)

"I really like those short skirts you've been wearing." (Inappropriate)

Difficult-to-Appreciate Coworkers and Troublesome Situations

What about that coworker you heartily dislike? How do you appreciate a coworker who is always borrowing your stapler and never returning it, or the colleague who takes credit for your ideas, or the coworker who got the promotion you deserved by kissing up to the boss?

Appreciation is more of a challenge in these circumstances, but it is worth going for, because it can change your experience of that very coworker. For example, ask yourself what you can value and be grateful for in the coworker who borrows your stapler. It's certainly not her failure to return the stapler. But your coworker does not spend her entire day borrowing and failing to return your stapler; she does many other things and has many other attributes. For the moment, put the stapler situation on hold, and actively work on appreciating and expressing appreciation to this coworker, in specific and genuine terms. For example, let her know that her good humor lightens your day, or that her idea made a project easier for you. Don't even think about your stapler.

As you emit a heartfelt vibration of appreciation, your experience of this coworker will shift. Either she will stop borrowing your stapler, or start returning it, or something entirely different will happen, such as a transfer to another department. Whatever the outcome, one thing is sure: your vibration of appreciation will link up with something about that coworker for you to appreciate, even if it ends up being her leaving the department.

How can appreciation help you to transform a painful work situation? For example, how can you work appreciation to your benefit with a boss who takes you to task for a piece of work that you did? Chris, a PR firm accounts representative and AG member, tells how:

> The company I work for is very busy, always lots going on, and I end up getting instructions from three or four different people on the same project. They'll just fly into my cubicle and drop a note on my desk, or leave a message on the voice mail; half the time I have to piece together what they're talking about. Well, I was putting together a presentation for a client, with all the input from everybody, and I thought that one person had told me, "You must give the dollar amount to the client at the time of the presentation," which I thought was unusual, but I did what they wanted. I made sure the amount was included in the presentation. Well, my main boss had a fit. He lit into me, saying that I should know better than to include it, and now the client would probably reject the proposal, and I'd better be able to clean the situation up.
>
> Apparently the person had said, "You must not give the dollar amount to the client at the time of the presentation," and I'd misheard it on the voice mail. I was devastated. I'd never been reprimanded like that, and I thought, "How can I turn this around? I have to keep working with my boss, I can't just run and hide. What do I do?"
>
> And I thought, "Well, I'll try using appreciation, what do I have to lose?" So I thought, "OK, I can appreciate that my boss's anger really

comes from his dedication to the company; he wants to do well for the company, and I can appreciate that."

And oddly enough, that calmed me down, made me feel better, less defensive. Then I thought, "I can appreciate that I'm upset because I like doing a good job. I pride myself on doing a good job." And that made me feel better too. Somehow, working with appreciation made the whole thing seem less personal, made it possible for me to pick up and keep going in a good direction.

Appreciation can also help you deal with unhappy clients and customers. Instead of focusing on how miserable they make your life, focus on what you can appreciate about that person. Stacey, an AG member, is a customer service representative for a computer company, so she knows about frustrated and unhappy customers. Here's what she found when she started reacting to them with appreciation:

My whole day is about people complaining about one thing or another that's not working with their computer. Most of the time, people are pretty nice about it, but sometimes I'll get a customer who's really irate. They're mad the computer won't do what they want it to do, so they're yelling at me. I used to get upset and I'd be cold with them. It's hard to stay warm and friendly like you're supposed to when someone's mad at you.

So the other day this lady calls, and she's having a fit because her computer won't recognize her printer, and she can't print anything out. Well, this time I decide to try appreciating, even though I'm upset and wish she'd stop yelling. All I could think was to say inside myself, "I appreciate you, I appreciate you" to this lady, even while I'm asking her for the information I need so I can help her. And suddenly it comes to me that the reason this lady is so upset is that she loves this computer and what it can do for her.

I found myself appreciating how much she loves her computer, and that changed the whole thing for me. I told her I could see how she'd be upset, that she must value her computer and what it usually does for her, and she sort of stopped in the middle of complaining and said, "Well, yes, I do," and then she was a lot calmer and I was able to complete the call feeling good about it. It was wild.

Do you want to see your sales go through the roof? Do you want to see yourself get raises and promotions? Do you want to see your business flourish? Then appreciate what you offer, be it a product or a service, and appreciate those who purchase and use it. People sense when you truly appreciate yourself, your product, or your service, and are attracted to you by virtue of the vibration you create. Your appreciation has a bonus: it encourages you to be your very best and to do your job at your highest level of ability. Such an attitude inevitably contributes to success.

When you deeply, wholeheartedly appreciate your clients or customers, they know it. And a fake smile doesn't cut it; vibration cannot be fooled. Everybody knows that the stereotypical used car salesman's smile and friendliness are a front. His vibration, usually one of disdain for his "marks," attracts a vibrational match: people hold him in low regard.

Think highly of your clients and customers. Value them. Be grateful to them not just for their purchase of your product or service, but for who they are as human beings. Let their well-being matter to you. Be grateful for how you contribute to their well-being with your product or service. Send out a powerful vibration of appreciation and you will readily attract like appreciation of yourself and your product or service. Your success is the natural vibrational consequence of your appreciation.

Appreciation Tips for the Workplace

1. *Appreciation Warm-Ups*

At the beginning of your day, set yourself up vibrationally for a successful day by doing a three- to five-minute "appreciation warm-up." Depending on the nature of your work and your preference, do your warm-up at home; in the car, bus, or train; or at your workplace, as you organize yourself for the day ahead.

The warm-up has three parts: first, review briefly what you generally appreciate about your work; then, decide what you intend to appreciate specifically about the day ahead; finally, describe what you appreciate about yourself and your contribution to the day.

Some people do this silently, with their eyes closed, while others prefer to say it aloud, or write it down in journal form.

AG member Diane manages a restaurant. Here's what she says about her appreciation warm-up:

> Usually I start by being grateful that I have this job; that I get to work at something I like. I think a little about how much I appreciate working with people, and being able to make their mealtime as pleasant as possible. I think about the staff, and how I appreciate their good work. Then I focus on appreciating all the people that will come in to eat today. I appreciate myself, and that I'm good at what I do, and am grateful that I'll be able to deal with whatever comes up, and something always comes up in the restaurant trade. When I do my appreciating thing

before I go in, that makes my whole day start off better. I used to go in all worried, and just get more worried throughout the day. Now I don't worry as much and things seem to go better. It's nice.

2. Appreciation Breaks

Whenever you take a coffee break, restroom break, lunch break, or any other kind of break, take an appreciation break at the same time. As you sip your coffee or wash your hands, just ask yourself, "What can I appreciate right here, right now?"

Sometimes it's as simple as "I'm really grateful for this break!" Sometimes it's something like, "I appreciate what a good day I'm having," or "I appreciate that I worked that thing out with my supervisor this morning," or "I appreciate that I'm really coming up with good ideas today."

It doesn't matter what you appreciate. Focusing on what you value and are grateful for will amplify your general feeling of appreciation about your work. Your confidence and feelings of worth in the workplace will increase significantly. You will feel connected to your purpose and the significance of what you do. You'll feel more effective. All of these will add up to your being more successful.

3. Appreciation Wrap-Up

Just as you started your work day with appreciation, take three to five minutes to end it with appreciation. Review the day and remember what you value and are grateful for. Make sure to include valuing yourself. After one week of doing this, Steve, an insurance agent and AG member, noticed a difference: "It felt kind of funny at first. I thought this is probably a waste of time, but OK. So on the way home I reviewed my day, and I was surprised at how many things I found to appreciate. It got me in a better mood, and I found that by the time I got home, I wasn't all stressed out like I usually am. My wife says I've been less grumpy all week. Guess it makes a difference. I didn't remember to appreciate myself though. I'll have to remember to do that this week."

Given that appreciation soothes your chaotic heart and brain rhythms and brings them into harmony, it makes sense that an appreciation wrap-up will help you end your day in a good mood. It also amplifies your general appreciation of work, bringing you more personal fulfillment and satisfaction.

Applying the Five Steps to a Work Scenario

Let's use the five steps to using appreciation for attracting a desired outcome in a situation that most of us will face at one time or another: wanting a promotion at work.

You're feeling overworked, undervalued, and underpaid. You have put in several times for a promotion, but you keep getting passed over. You complain to anyone who will listen about how unfair it is and how miserable you are, but that's not getting you anywhere. You're willing to give appreciation a try.

Step One: Choose What You Want to Transform or Attract

Your choice is already made. You want to be promoted to a specific position. Give form and reality to your choice by familiarizing yourself with the job's responsibilities and duties. Find out whom you would be working with, what the supervisor or other higher-ups are like, and what their unspoken rules are. The more you know the ins and outs of the position, the more clearly you will be able to appreciate it.

Step Two: Determine the Feelings behind Your Desire

What does this promotion mean to you? What is its value to you? Your first response might be, "A bigger paycheck," but ask yourself what it is about that bigger paycheck, specifically, that holds meaning for you. Is it the good feeling of paying your bills without juggling? The security of finally being able to put something aside in a savings account? Is it being able to remodel your aging kitchen, or to join the gym? Feel how thankful you will be for the benefits your bigger paycheck will bring to your life. The more clearly you articulate this, the easier it is to launch and hold a vibration of appreciation for that paycheck.

Think about other aspects of the promotion: What do the new responsibilities and duties mean to you? How will you feel about them? Do you value how you'll be using more of your skills and talents? Are you looking forward to learning new techniques and approaches, and tackling new and challenging projects? Are you eager to become part of a new team? Are you enthusiastic about your new coworkers and managers? Allow yourself to feel a deep sense of gratitude for all that your new position will bring you.

Step Three: Weed Out Conflicting Thoughts and Beliefs

Root out thoughts and beliefs that don't support your desire for a promotion. When you think of the promotion, what troubles you? For example:

Current Belief	**Changed Belief**
It'll never happen; I'll just get passed over again.	*Things change. I'm approaching getting this promotion differently; I can get different results.*
It's all in whom you know, and I don't know the right people.	*Other things matter than just whom you know. This time my skills and qualities will make a difference.*
People are so used to seeing me in my current position, they don't think of me any other way.	*My job now is not the whole of who I am. I can show more of what I'm capable of, so that people will think of me differently.*

Once you've zeroed in on the thoughts and beliefs that might obstruct your launching a focused vibration, create affirmations to help you stay clear and focused, such as:

- I am always at the right place at the right time.
- I have what it takes to get what I want.
- Success comes to me easily and joyously.

Repeat your affirmations often, with passion and zeal!

Step Four: Launch Your Vibration of Appreciation

Appreciating what you've got is always how you should start building your vibration of appreciation for a new desire. Even if you hate your current position, look at it with new eyes. What can you appreciate about it? What value does your position bring to you? Consider what your position has brought you in the past. Be grateful for the skills you have learned, people you have met, experiences you have had. In one way or another, these have all contributed to your well-being.

Do not think about the downsides of your current position. Whenever you think, "I can't stand that coworker" or "Paperwork drives me buggy," let the thought go and soothe yourself with appreciation for some portion of your work, however small. Stay focused by reminding yourself why you're exercising such self-restraint: to keep your vibration of appreciation for the new position as strong as possible.

Get ready to launch your vibration of appreciation for the new position. Find that quiet, relaxing place both in your environment and within yourself, and relax. Gather your thoughts and feelings of appreciation for the new position. Think about the many joys your promotion will bring: the financial joys, the workplace joys, the personal joys. Let the feelings of happiness and gratitude for these joys flood your whole being, as your vibration of appreciation builds. Once the vibration feels strong and focused, feel it as intensely as you can for three to five minutes, savoring the good feelings that wash through you. Then relax, and go about the rest of your day, basking in appreciation.

When you go back the next day, and the next, and the next, to that same old job, resist the temptation to become bitter or demoralized. Remind yourself that it takes time for your vibration to sort out other vibrations, and align itself appropriately for your success. Trust the process, and stay true to your valuing and being grateful, keeping your vibration of appreciation strong.

Step Five: Work Your Appreciation

Start looking for that promotion's arrival. It may come in the form of a training seminar offered to upper management that somehow intrigues you, even though you're not upper management. You take action by asking if you can listen in on the seminar, and your interest in improving yourself catches the eye of the powers that be. Or it may come in the form of a coworker's need for help, where your willingness to volunteer puts you one step ahead of whoever else is competing for the promotion.

Maybe you think of a way to streamline a task, and you take the initiative to write up a report on it. Perhaps you get inspired to join Toastmasters or the Rotarians, and find yourself becoming friends with people who have influence. Maybe you start to walk into work with a confident attitude, lose the complaining, and impress management with your new upbeat manner. Whatever the avenues through which your promotion starts to come, be ready to seize the opportunity and follow through on what feels right to you. Inspiration is the motivator, but action is the key.

Work, and everything associated with it—your coworkers, customers, clients, bosses, your salary, promotions, and all the rest—give you a wonderful opportunity to apply your appreciative skills. No longer will you view work as a drudgery. Instead, appreciation gives you the tools, confidence, and motivation to make of work what it was always supposed to be: a source of happiness, success, and fulfillment.

8

Your Children and   Appreciation

A pint-sized seven-year-old cries as he runs from classmates calling him "sissy" and "chicken."

A ten-year-old is back in the principal's office for the umpteenth time, after hitting another kid and stealing his lunch money.

A thirteen-year-old, staring at a blackboard full of incomprehensible numbers, figures that running with a gang sounds pretty cool.

A dejected fourteen-year-old moons over the photograph of her betraying boyfriend and contemplates cutting herself or going for the big one—slitting her wrists.

An angry sixteen-year-old, repeatedly snubbed and rejected by his schoolmates for the unconventional way he looks and dresses, opens fire in the cafeteria.

These situations appear completely different, ranging from the most mundane to the most extreme, yet all these children have one thing in common: they suffer from lack of appreciation. They fail to value themselves, fail to value others, or fail to value life itself. In the absence of valuing, they are hardly likely to be grateful for anything, and so they are not able to appreciate.

When a child is appreciated, however, and taught to appreciate, amazing things happen. For example, here's the story of what happened to a group of children in a severely disadvantaged urban area of Worcester, Massachusetts, home of Clark University, as reported in a 2003 *Los Angeles Times* article.

Historically, the local residents and the university population had eyed each other with a mutual animosity so great that Clark officials were seriously considering moving the university out of the city. After a number of traditional and unsuccessful attempts at improving relations, officials at Clark realized that something different had to be done, something to address the underlying reasons for the impoverished and dismal conditions of their shared neighborhood. Their solution was to create a new public high school with free tuition across the street from the university, and hire a dedicated educator from that very neighborhood, Donna Rodrigues, to run the school. The officials stated that they had "faith in the kids and faith in the neighborhood," which are but other words for *appreciation* of the kids and the neighborhood.

Appreciation was a theme in every aspect of the endeavor. Children attending the new school were quickly taught to appreciate their school and each other: no bullying or street talk was allowed. The staff showed its appreciation of the students by setting high expectations for them, and by giving help and guidance to meet those expectations. Classes were small, teachers put in long hours, and a constant stream of student teachers from the university were there to assist the students.

The results are undisputed. Six years after its inception in 1997, every member of the first graduating class, almost all of whom came from very poor families where little if any English was spoken, passed the tough state achievement test with ease, and all plan to attend college, which heretofore would have been considered an impossibility. In addition to that, crime and other problems of urban blight have decreased in the surrounding area.

Such is the power of appreciation.

Don and Jeanne Elium, in their book *Raising a Son*, talk about the power of appreciation, which they harnessed by naming the qualities that they admired in a child:

> To many tribal peoples the world over, a son's unique soul origin has to be carefully identified by specified adults. This soulful dimension of the boy was praised, honored [appreciated], and developed over time.
>
> If he was shy and fascinated by his inner world of thoughts, feelings, and dreams, he might be known as "He Who Looks Inward." Perhaps he was not the fiercest warrior, but when a fellow warrior was depressed or emotionally confused, he would go to "He Who Looks Inward" for help in sorting out his troubles. This second "name" brought forth a boy's dominant qualities in the most meaningful and positive light...
>
> When I first met John, he was thirteen. I feared that his "second name" was "Boy Who Destroys All Adults' Sanity." He had a string of probation officers, counselors, teachers, and social workers a mile long behind him.
>
> After a long time of trust-building between us, I finally put it to him as clearly as I could. I called him "powerful." Then I told him, "You move mountains when you want to. Your only problem is that you keep moving them *in* your way instead of out of your way."... This became our running joke: "What mountains have you moved in your way this

week, and what mountains have you moved out of your way?" In time, John learned how to stay out of needless trouble and to create a life more of his choosing.... "He Who Moves Mountains" is now applying to law school.

As this example shows, appreciation empowers children and moves them from feeling victimized and helpless to feeling strong and self-confident. By naming and appreciating their strengths, we support the full realization of their unique gifts and talents.

Appreciation cannot solve all of our kids' problems and dilemmas, for life is more complex than that. What it can do, however, is provide a critical foundation that gives children the potential for joy, and the wherewithal to face life's challenges more successfully. This foundation has three cornerstones: appreciation of self, appreciation of others, and appreciation of life. The table on the next page shows how each is critical in a child's development.

Appreciating Your Child: The Early Years

Your children's ability to appreciate themselves, other people, and the world starts with you, their parents. Whether you're a mom and dad, a single parent, or a foster parent, if you are caring for a child in the early years, you are the biggest influence in that child's life.

Your children learn to appreciate themselves, others, and the world through your example. At the most basic level, when you appreciate your children, you let them know that simply by existing they have value and worth, they matter, and that you are grateful for their existence.

Dr. Edward Shafranske, Professor of Clinical Psychology, Pepperdine University, put it sweetly in a 1988 interview: "When we're babies in the crib, what

Appreciation	Quality Developed	Results
Appreciation of self	*Feeling valued for one's very being*	*Empowerment, self-confidence; a core belief in one's abilities; inner security; decrease in fear-based beliefs and actions*
Appreciation of others	*Empathy; respect for others' existence, regardless of what they do or have*	*The ability to cooperate, negotiate, seek constructive solutions even in the face of disagreement or conflict; decrease in bigotry, prejudice, hatred, and violence*
Appreciation of life	*A profound sense of connection with nature, other people, all creation; an ability to see the bigger picture*	*Flexibility, an ability to ride the ups and downs of life, to accept change; willingness to collaborate for the greater good*

we really need is for Mom or Dad to look at us in the morning when we're waking up and say 'Oh, you're up! How wonderful! You're awake!' in that sort of lovely baby voice. And there it is. That as we're born, we're appreciated, treasured, and that Mom is happy and Dad is happy just because we're awake."

A baby has little self-awareness. She discovers who she is and learns whether she has value through your eyes, reactions, and responses. For example, when your baby, gurgling with delight, points to the mobile above her crib and you join in with joyous baby talk of your own, you validate her experience of joy with your own joyous response. When you do this, you let her know that her experience, and thus her existence, is valuable.

When you tickle your baby's tummy during play, amplifying his delight, you are not only mirroring and validating his experience, you are attuning to your child's emotions and reflecting them back to him in a positive way.

Dr. Allan Schore, psychologist and neurobiological researcher, describes in *Affect Regulation and the Origin of the Self* how this process of mirroring, validating, and attuning has been found to directly impact a child's brain development, promoting healthy circuitry in the right orbitofrontal cortex—an area that plays a role in many higher brain functions, such as the ability to self-reflect, empathize, and develop moral behaviors.

When there are structural deficits or damage to the orbitofrontal cortex, people tend to have an inability to be empathic. Empathy, the ability to put yourself in another person's shoes, is lacking in sociopathic individuals who can depersonalize and hurt others without regard for the pain they cause. Without empathy, it is easy to feel contempt for, and therefore do harm to, others.

Clearly, the development of a healthy brain involves more than genetics. Dr. Schore's research shows that the structural organs of the brain and functional aspects of brain circuitry (the "hardwiring" of the brain) depend, especially during the first two years of life, on a parent's ability to understand and regulate a child's feelings and needs.

High levels of shared positive emotions between baby and parents during the tenth to thirteenth months of life, Dr. Schore notes, are critical to the creation of permanent pathways for joy in the child's brain circuitry. Most parents instinctively know how to share positive emotions with their babies, in ways as simple as these:

• Your baby smiles at you. You smile back and say "What a happy boy!"

- You are nursing your infant. You catch her eye and look lovingly back at her.
- Your toddler is feverish and cranky. You soothe him by rocking him and rhythmically repeating, "I know, I know."
- Your toddler takes her first steps toward you alone. You hold out your arms and catch her with excited congratulations: "Look at you! You did it! You walked to Mommy all by yourself!"

For children, appreciation is not a luxury. It is fundamental to the healthy development of their brain, to their mental and emotional thriving, and to their future happiness and success.

Appreciating Your Child: The Growing Years

For most of us, appreciating our children is instinctive. This is easiest when your child is being adorable. However, as any parent will attest, from birth to adulthood, adorable is regularly interspersed with fussy, difficult, irritating, obnoxious, or downright impossible. That's when appreciation can fly out the window.

The unfortunate message to our children can be, "You're only valuable when you're being adorable. I am not grateful for your existence when you're being other than who I want you to be." Appreciation then becomes tied to approval, a dangerous message, for it tells your child that he has no intrinsic value, and that his value depends upon his behaviors, feelings, and desires coinciding with what you deem acceptable.

The challenge—and it is a challenge!—is to empower your child's unique self, while helping her grow up to be responsible, accountable, and well-functioning.

For example, your two-year-old is methodically removing every pot and pan from the cabinet and banging away on them with great glee and abandon. You are helpless to stop him, as you're on the phone, trying to conduct a particularly delicate piece of business. You're not feeling appreciative at all. In fact, your irritation and frustration are mounting by the second, so that by the time you get off the phone, all you can do is yell, "No, bad boy!" while you scoop your baby up and dump him in his playpen, to wail away in solitary misery. Now your baby is feeling worthless. His beautiful exploration of sound had no value for you, and therefore he believes he has no value for you.

With appreciation, the scenario would unfold differently. You would feel the same frustration (you're only human), but before you interacted with your baby, you would take a deep breath to calm yourself. Then, as you lifted your baby away from the pans, you'd say something like "You are a wonderful drummer; you can make such loud music!" By finding something to appreciate—that your baby has created his own play—you convey to him that he is valued. You generate as much of a real feeling of appreciation for your baby's energetic banging as possible, matching what you say with hugs and kisses and other delighted expressions. Even if you remove him from the pots and pans, he won't suffer from a lack of worth.

During their teen years, our children push our frustration and aggravation buttons probably more than at any other stage of their development. They are doing their best to differentiate themselves from us; often it seems that they choose the exactly opposite behavior from what we find acceptable. Like toddlers, rational thought often seems lacking, but the difference is that now the tantrums are bigger.

For example, your teenager is desperate to go to a party. You say no because you have family plans.

Your teenager yells, "I hate you! You never let me do what I want."

You may respond, "What are you talking about? I let you do all sorts of things you want—just last weekend you got to go to a slumber party, didn't you?"

With this reply, you are being logical, but your teen doesn't see it that way. She just sees you as being obstructionist, as not understanding.

"You're horrible! I hate you!" she shouts as she sulks away, feeling unloved, unworthy, and most certainly unappreciated.

If, instead, you acknowledge that this party has value for your child, a very different discussion might take place. Look for something to appreciate in what your child wants, and you might find yourself saying, "You really care about going to this party."

Your teenager's response may be, "Duh!"

Still hanging on to your appreciative mindset, you could say, "Talk to me about why this party is important to you."

Your teenager would no doubt sigh, and say, "Everyone's going to be there, Mom. I don't want to be left out." Your child is telling you why this event matters.

You can then validate what she finds worthwhile by saying, "Belonging is really important to you." Instead of defending your own position, you've appreciated what is valuable about your teen's desire. By respecting what she finds valuable, you've given her the subconscious message that she is valuable. From there, problem solving becomes a whole different matter, for you have also lined up a vibration of appreciation that can align with your child's vibration of appreciation. Cooperation is now possible.

"Let's see if we can find a way for you not to be left out," would be the beginning of your finding a solution together that respects your values and hers, and for which both of you will feel grateful.

Appreciating your child teaches your child to appreciate himself, opening wide the doors to his future happiness and success. Self-appreciation is intimately linked to self-worth, which is the basis for self-confidence, self-empowerment, and the development of a core belief in one's ability to be and do in the world.

A child who doesn't learn to appreciate herself will lack self-worth. A child who doesn't believe that she is worth much may be overly reliant on others' approval, and may be hurt, even devastated, by their disapproval. This child gives up on herself easily. She doesn't know the self within her that's worth hanging in there for.

A child who doesn't value himself doesn't recognize that he has strengths that offset his weaknesses. He generalizes from one failure, such as a difficulty with math, to believing himself to be a failure. He generalizes from one rebuff, such as a classmate hollering out, "Hey dork-face," to a total rejection of self: "I'm not worth anything."

The upshot is a child who functions far below his potential. He manifests his unhappiness with himself by asocial behaviors, such as not applying himself in school, whining a lot, or acting moody, sullen, or uncooperative. A "smart mouth" or temper tantrums may also be present. This child is nowhere near achieving the happiness and success in life that is possible for him.

A sense of worth is so important to our psychological existence that children will seek it out wherever and however they can get it, whether it is a gang, a cult, a boyfriend, drugs, or an alter ego, such as "Mr. Cool," "Ms. Slut," "Miss Hoity Toity," or "Wild One." Even a negative sense of worth is better than no sense of worth.

Helping Your Child Learn Self-Appreciation

How do you help your child achieve a positive sense of worth? By teaching him how to appreciate himself. Do this by:

1. *First, no matter how your child is behaving, find something within him to value and be grateful for.*
2. *Then, point out to your child the specific quality or action you are appreciating about him.*

This is especially important when your child is having a tough time and might naturally put himself down. For example, he is laboring over his multiplication tables. Tongue firmly wedged in the corner of his mouth, he applies himself with all his might. After ten minutes, he gives up, laying his head down on the kitchen table, staring at nothing while he picks at the loose Formica at the edge of the table.

Resist the urge to say, "Stop that! Sit up straight and do your homework!" Instead, sit by him and say, "What's not working here?"

He grumbles, "I don't know. I can't do this. It's too hard."

You nod, buying time.

What can you appreciate in this situation? You think back to a time when your child was challenged, but persevered. You say, "Remember that science project with the worms you did last year?"

"Yeah," your child mutters.

"Remember how hard it was for you," you continue, "but how you stuck with it? And finally you figured it out and got a big fat gold star for it?"

"Yeah," your child says, a little less miserably.

"You're really good at that," you say.

'What?" he asks.

"Sticking it out," you reply.

"Yeah?" your son asks, shyly pleased.

"Yeah," you reply. "You are a mighty sticker-outer. You stick with things and, gosh darn it, you see them through. That's a really good thing to be."

"Huh," your son replies, lifting his head up and picking up his pencil.

"So, let's you and I work on this multiplication thing together," you say. "And you be the really great sticker-outer you are, and you'll end up with a gold star again."

"Yeah," he says, "OK." And you're off and running.

Keep reminding your child what a great "sticker-outer" he is whenever he flags, and through the power of your appreciation, he discovers something to appreciate about himself. Over time, he'll internalize the qualities and attributes you point out to him, appreciating them fully himself, thereby being able to successfully and joyously cope with the challenges of life.

Why It's Important for Your Child to Appreciate Others

With a sense of his own value and of being appreciated, a child finds it easier to appreciate others' value. Appreciation for other people—valuing human life itself—keeps a child from harming others.

It's easy to show your child how to value and be grateful for the others in his life. The best place to start is at home, with the family. Every day brings many opportunities.

For example, your child comes running to you, crying that his brother took his toy. Your instinctive reaction might be, "I'm sorry, sweetie, but it's no big deal. Go play with another toy." Or you may reprimand your other son for taking the toy.

Working with appreciation, you might respond differently. To the child who came crying to you, you might say, "I'm sorry, sweetie; your brother can be a pain sometimes, but I know you both like playing together. I've seen you work things out with him before. How about trying that now?" To the son who took the toy, you might say, "I know you appreciate playing with your brother, even though it's not looking that way right now. Can you figure out a way to share?"

Get your children in the habit of appreciating others by making appreciation a part of your regular routine. For example, put a sheet up on the refrigerator entitled: "Things to appreciate about us!" Divide the sheet into columns, and print each family member's name at the top of a column. Each person writes down something they appreciate about each other person, and initials their entry. The object is not to receive the most appreciation, but to give the most appreciation. At the end of the week, whoever wrote the most appreciative comments gets a special treat.

When you jot down something to appreciate, tie it to a personality trait, which provides the recipient with the bonus of seeing how others enjoy his or her qualities and talents. Here's an example:

I appreciate my child's

- cooperativeness (shared his Nintendo)
- good nature (pitched in without being asked)
- sense of humor (made me laugh and uplifted me)
- honesty (gave my dropped change to me)
- self-discipline (homework handed in on time)

Teach your child by being a living example of appreciation. Children are born imitators; they model their behavior on the adults around them. They will imitate anything, including your appreciation of others—or lack of it.

Make a habit of appreciating the sales clerk, UPS driver, mail carrier, home room teacher, and other people your children watch you interact with. Be specific as you express your gratitude for the clerk's helpful suggestions, or the mail carrier's punctuality, or the home room teacher's creative assignments. Your children will learn to do the same. Watching appreciation in action is the best way for children to learn how to do it themselves.

Your children will learn that appreciating others is often a more effective way to accomplish their goals than manipulation, wheedling, whining, and arguing. Since appreciation has a vibration, your children's vibration of appreciation will automatically engage other people's increased willingness to cooperate with them. Point out the effectiveness of appreciation, and your children will be encouraged to use it more on their own.

Learning to Appreciate Life

Few experiences are as rewarding as teaching a child to appreciate life. Children are natural appreciators, eager to wonder and marvel. With guidance and support, they readily see the value in life and all things living.

Play the Appreciation Game with your children. For example, sit and watch a sunset with them. Ask, "What's great [of value] about the sunset?" See how many different things they can come up with. Or, as you're driving them to school, ask, "What's great about this drive?" Share with them what you think is great about the drive, and why you are grateful for it. As you do, you broaden your children's ideas about what it is to be valuable. As you express your gratitude, you show how easy it is to be grateful about many different things.

Any time is an opportunity to help children see what they can appreciate about the world around them. When you teach your children to work appreciation early in their lives, you give them a gift of true freedom: the freedom to choose and create for themselves lives full of joy, love, success, and abundance.

9

Appreciate Your Way to Health and Healing

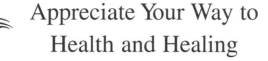

One of the great revelations in modern medicine was the discovery of the body-mind connection. How you perceive and interpret situations and people in your life, including yourself, impacts your physical body: your joy stimulates it in one way, your anger in a different way. As Deepak Chopra writes in *Ageless Body, Timeless Mind*, "In short, our bodies are the physical results of all the interpretations we have been learning to make since we were born."

Appreciation is biochemical. Your thoughts and feelings translate into the release of particular chemicals in your body, what Dr. Candace Pert, a research professor in physiology and biophysics at Georgetown University, calls "the molecules of emotion." For example, have you ever felt passive and physically immobilized after a negative interaction or emotion? As explained by Dr. Allan Schore in a 2001 article, your brain has produced the neurohormone cortisol, which tells your whole body to shut down and withdraw. Compare this with the experience of seeing a warm, appreciative face, or hearing the familiar voice of a loved one. When you experience positive interactions and emotions, the neurotransmitter dopamine and the hormone oxytocin are released into your brain. These chemicals, discussed by Dr. Uvnas-Moberg in a 1997 study, relax you into a sense of safety, and help you show up for your life in an active, motivated, even joyful way.

As Dr. Pert notes:

Your brain is extremely well integrated with the rest of your body at a molecular level, so much so that the term *mobile brain* is an apt description of the psychosomatic network through which intelligent information travels from one system to another. Every one of the zones, or systems, of the network—the neural, the hormonal, the gastrointestinal, and the immune—is set up to communicate with one another, via peptides and messenger-specific peptide receptors. Every second, a massive information exchange is occurring in your body . . . The neuropeptides and receptors, the biochemicals of emotion, are, as I have said, the messengers carrying information to link the major systems of the body into one unit that we can call the body-mind. We can no longer think of the emotions as having less validity than physical, material substance, but instead must see them as cellular signals that are involved in the process of translating information into physical reality, *literally transforming mind into matter* [emphasis added].

Dr. Pert describes how this close interaction between thought, emotion, and bodily systems explains why recent widows are twice as likely to develop breast cancer, and why chronically depressed individuals are four times more likely to get sick. The mental and emotional message of appreciation is carried to and benefits virtually every system of your body.

Reynolds, an AG member, shares his experience of how appreciation impacted his body and mind:

I'm a landscape gardener. I love working outdoors, which is a good thing considering what I do for a living. I've been at it about fifteen years. I've always been healthy and fit, until about a year and a half ago, when I started getting sinus infections. I'd get over one infection, only to get another a couple of weeks later.

When I started with the group a year ago or so, I decided to tackle these darned infections. I kept hearing how "what you think and what you feel impacts your health," so I thought, "OK, what am I thinking about here? What's different in the last six months?" And then it hit me—my boss! My old boss retired about then, his son took over, and let me tell you, his son is nothing like the old man. He wants me to clock in and clock out, I have to check off lists when I take out and return equipment, I have to write down problems I had with anything—a gardener, a client, a tree, anything. I even have to write mileage down to the exact tenth of a mile. I realized I wasn't appreciating my work any more. I was hardly even seeing the plants I was working with, much less admiring their growth and the results of my landscaping. I was miserable coming in to work and miserable leaving it.

So I decided to accept that my boss had new ways of going about things, and I set that whole thing in the back of my mind. I just quit thinking about it, and instead made myself look at my plants and appreciate them the way I used to. I focused on what I love about working outdoors. I made lists of stuff to appreciate about my work, and read them over and over. Well, it took a little while, but sure enough, my sinus infections got fewer and fewer. I haven't had one now in about nine, ten months. But if I let myself get bothered by one of my boss's rules and regulations my sinuses start to act up again, and it reminds me, real quick, to get back on that appreciation path.

Appreciation can be used specifically to help you get and stay well. Take the common cold. Most of us bemoan its arrival: "Oh, no, I have a cold. This happens to me every winter. Here we go, I'll be sneezing and coughing until spring. I feel awful. Nothing ever makes it better. It's nice of John to bring over soup, but I'm sick to death of soup, and I don't believe that old wives' tale about chicken soup, anyway."

Your attention is understandably focused on how miserable you feel. You don't notice that most of your body's systems are working just fine; all you see is your cold. You don't notice how people and conditions around you are contributing to your recovery; all you allow yourself to see is what reinforces your current misery. Your negativity adds stress to your condition, making it harder for you to recover.

How can appreciation help you more effectively get rid of this sneezing, coughing, achy nuisance? By switching your focus from hating the cold, from thinking about how miserable you feel and how much you resent being laid low, to appreciating wellness. The power of a switch in focus, which has been repeatedly proven by placebo studies, can make the difference between a week of misery and a couple of days, if that, of mild discomfort.

A placebo is an inert or innocuous substance (such as a sugar pill) that has no treatment value whatsoever. People given a placebo often improve—not because of the contents of the placebo, but because they believe the pill will heal them. Their focus switches from how ill they are, to *how well the medicine will work*. It is this focus on wellness that results in healing. This change in focus has successfully killed pain, lowered blood pressure, stopped excessive gastric secretions in ulcer patients, and even led to remissions of advanced malignancy in cancer patients. When you focus on illness or injury, you emit a frequency of vibration that seeks to align with a like vibration, making it more difficult to heal. When you appreciate wellness, however, you emit a frequency of vibration that aligns with a vibration of well-being, thereby facilitating your healing.

Focusing on wellness is not the same as denying illness. Denial says, "It's all in your head." Focusing on wellness says, "It's all in your vibration." Your vibration is composed of how you think and feel. When you think and feel appreciation, you transform your perception and interpretation of the world inside and outside of you into positive, life-supporting events.

For example, denial would say, "I don't have a cold," as you sneeze, cough, and hack your way miserably through your day. Denial won't work, because you can't believe you don't have a cold. The evidence is right there with you. When you focus on appreciation, you don't deny anything. On the contrary, you start by acknowledging the reality: "I'm sneezing and coughing, I probably have a cold." Then you move on to appreciate whatever you can in order to help yourself heal.

Think how your experience of a cold might differ when you focus on appreciating:

- I can appreciate how long it's been since I last had a cold. I can hardly even remember the last time.
- I can value and be grateful for how fast I tend to heal. I can appreciate how quickly I usually get over colds.
- I can appreciate how well this new cough medicine is working.
- I can appreciate John stopping by with soup. I can appreciate the warmth of the broth and the love with which he made it.

- I can appreciate how the rest of my body still functions beautifully: my digestion still works, my blood still circulates, my heart beats. All of these other parts of me are wonderfully well.

As you focus on thoughts and feelings of genuine appreciation, fueled by your intention to get well, your attention is geared towards health. Your perceptions and interpretations change: you no longer perceive yourself as a runny nose with legs, you perceive yourself as a whole being, with one small ailing portion that you are encouraging to recover. You interpret situations such as your friend stopping by as valuable contributions to your well-being.

Now your thoughts, feelings, perceptions, and interpretations are aligning with a vibration of wellness. The result will be experiences of wellness that will match up with your vibration and be attracted to you.

Rx for Healing with Appreciation

Appreciating wellness can do much more than accelerate the healing of a cold. Appreciation can be used dynamically as part of your overall approach to healing, and to achieving wellness. Change your health focus with appreciation by following these four steps:

1. Focus on Wellness

Begin creating a general vibration of good health by appreciating the ordinary wellness of your extraordinary body. Pay attention to how you talk to yourself when you are well and thriving. Do you even notice your body when you're feeling fine? Take time on a regular basis to express your appreciation to your body. Tell it how much you value and are grateful for its amazing, continuous good functioning.

If you think talking to your body is silly, just monitor your thoughts for a few days and you'll realize that you talk to your body all the time, only mostly in unappreciative, critical terms. Here are some examples:

- "Shoot, indigestion again. My stomach's a mess. Can't eat hardly anything without hurting."
- "My feet hurt; look at that bunion, it's gross."
- "My face is all broken out. I thought that was supposed to end at adolescence. I hate this."

Nowhere is there an acknowledgment of how often your stomach digests just fine; or how your feet support you and move in the correct ways for you to walk; or how 99 percent of your face is acne free, and how it laughs, pouts, and grimaces without your having to do anything about it. So, change how you talk to your body: appreciate what works, instead of continuously focusing on what doesn't. When you do this, you'll reinforce your body's current health and well-being.

2. Establish Wellness-Oriented Beliefs

Some beliefs contribute to an appreciation of wellness, and some sabotage wellness. To determine your beliefs, answer the following questions. Then look at the answer key to see which of your beliefs support an appreciation of wellness, and which don't.

1. *Do you believe that your natural state of being is one of health?   Yes / No*
2. *Do you believe that you should feel well and full of energy most of the time?   Yes / No*

3. *Do you believe that healing is an arduous process, requiring a great deal of energy and outside assistance under most circumstances?   Yes / No*

4. *Do you believe that healing is something the body does quite naturally, requiring outside assistance some of the time?   Yes / No*

5. *Do you believe that health automatically declines with age?   Yes / No*

6. *Do you believe that illness saps your vital energy or diminishes your capacities, so that each time you are ill, you are less likely to recover fully from the next illness?   Yes / No*

7. *Do you believe that doctors are always right?   Yes / No*

8. *Do you believe that there are innumerable ways to approach any given ailment or injury?   Yes / No*

9. *Do you believe that, if you are getting worse from a given ailment, you are irrevocably doomed to getting worse and worse?   Yes / No*

Answer Key: 1. Y, 2. Y, 3. N, 4. Y, 5. N, 6. N, 7. N, 8. Y, 9. N

Compare your answers to the quiz with those in the Answer Key, which are based on an appreciative approach to wellness. Using this comparison as a starting point, comb through your beliefs on health and healing, and eliminate those that do not contribute to an appreciation of wellness. Remember, a belief is simply a habit of thought, something you repeat to yourself regularly and frequently. Choose beliefs that serve you, and repeat them to yourself until wellness-oriented beliefs become your new habit of thought.

3. Replace Your Self-Pity with Self-Comfort

It's normal when you're sick or injured to feel sorry for yourself. After all, something not very pleasant is happening to you, and self-pity can soothe you to a degree. The problem comes not from transitory feelings of self-pity, but when you dwell on "poor me." The more you cling to self-pity, the less effective your vibration will be in aligning with wellness, and the more you may prolong your illness or injury.

What you are really looking for are ways to give yourself extra attention and pampering. Release your self-pity by finding good-feeling alternatives, such as:

- Instead of, "Oh, poor me, I've got this runny nose and I ache all over, I think I'll have ice cream," say, "What can I appreciate right now? What would make me feel better? I think I'll have some ice cream."
- Instead of, "Poor me, I feel so awful, I can't stand the phone, why do people have to call, that ringing hurts my ears," say, "What would I appreciate here? I'd really value some peace and quiet. I think I'll turn the phone ringer off. Ahhhh, that's nice."

Here are some other pity-busting ways to comfort yourself:

- Listen to soothing music
- Keep a supply of chicken soup on hand
- Listen to an audiobook, read a book, or watch a TV show that soothes, uplifts, or helps you mentally escape
- Have clean pajamas on hand
- Take a bath with healing herbs and pleasing scents
- Spend time on the phone with an especially nurturing friend

4. Ask Yourself "What Can I Appreciate in this Situation?"

Whether you're well or not, constantly look for things to appreciate about your body and your health. When you ask, "What can I appreciate in this situation?" you generate an even stronger vibration of wellness.

Remember to be truthful with yourself—vibration is never fooled. Don't say "I can appreciate..." until you've found something you can legitimately appreciate. You may have to start small: "I can appreciate that my little toe isn't hurting." Whether you build your appreciation of wellness bit by bit, or chunk by chunk, just do it. The more you do it, the easier it gets, and the more intense and powerful your vibration of appreciation becomes, resulting in further alignment with experiences of wellness.

We can learn appreciation from disabled persons, many of whom clearly demonstrate that they are simply "differently abled." They compensate for their disabilities and live highly functioning physical lives, even as they accommodate wheelchairs, prosthetics, or missing body parts and senses. For example, 80 percent of the patients at the ICRC Orthopedic Center in Kabul, Afghanistan, are land-mine victims needing prostheses. Eighty-five percent of the staff are amputees, too. For them, the first step in learning to live life differently abled is appreciation. The Center's director, Alberto Cairo, said in a 2002 *Los Angeles Times* article, "I tell them to stop thinking about what they have lost, and to think only about what is now possible... Some say this is such a sad place, I say no, no, this is a very, very happy place. This is where life begins again."

Appreciation for the abilities they do have allows differently abled individuals to lead full, rich lives.

Because emotions originate in both your mind and your body, focusing on thoughts and feelings of appreciation results in an ever-increasing upward spiral of wellness. As Dr. Pert writes in *Molecules of Emotion*, "Do emotions originate in the head or the body? Both. It's simultaneous—a two-way street. Every change in the physiological state is accompanied by an appropriate change in the mental-emotional state, conscious or unconscious, and vice versa."

Appreciation Diminishes Stress

Another way that appreciation directly contributes to health is by diminishing stress. Childre and Martin note in *The HeartMath Solution*:

> Appreciation is a powerful force. It eats the stress response for breakfast. You can be confident that as you focus on sincere feelings of appreciation, your nervous system will naturally come into balance. Biologically, all of the systems in your body, including your brain, will work in greater harmony. The electromagnetic field radiating from your body will resonate with the ordered, coherent pattern emitted by your heart. And every cell in your system will benefit.

As your body's systems work harmoniously together, the harmful effects of stress are lessened. Your immune system functions more effectively, helping you achieve and maintain good health. In addition, when you perceive and interpret the world around you through an appreciative frame of mind, you no longer perceive situations and events as only or primarily stressful. As Charlene, a kindergarten teacher's aide and AG member, tells us:

> I hurt my lower back from playing with the children, moving equipment around, and from all the other physical activity my job entails. My doctor was very strict with my restrictions. He told me I had to stop even moderate physical activity while he attempted to rehabilitate my lower back, "or else you'll wind up needing surgery"—which I really didn't want.
>
> I agreed to follow his orders, but frankly I was horribly depressed. I felt unproductive and useless. The kids would want to tussle and I couldn't; they'd want me to move a tricycle or lift them up and I couldn't;

I couldn't even let them run into me to get hugs. It was awful. I had ferocious headaches at the end of every day. I would cry myself to sleep and not want to get up in the morning.

Well, the group helped me think about my limitations differently. They encouraged me to appreciate what I can do, not dwell on what I can't. They helped me get creative with how I did things. I realized I could hug the kids just fine from a sitting down position, so I didn't have to give up hugging them. I got them to help me move the tricycles and other things by making a game of it, so I did more directing and they did more pushing—and giggling. I taught them how to use boxes for steps to climb over stuff I used to lift them over. I found all sorts of ways of doing my job I'd never thought of before—all from looking at "OK, what can I do, what is of value here?" instead of "I'm broken, I can do nothing of value." My headaches are pretty much gone, and I feel good about myself. What a relief!

The less you see what happens to you (or in your world) as a threat, the less likely you are to suffer the damages of the stress response. For example, when you are suddenly faced with a problem, your immediate reaction may be fear. When your car breaks down, you may think, "I won't be able to get my car fixed." Or if you lose your job, your first thought likely would be, "How will I pay my bills?"

Fear increases stress levels, decreasing the efficiency of your immune system over time. You are then more susceptible to colds, illnesses, and infections, and not as able to recover. An increase in stress also adversely impacts your basic processes: breathing, digestion, metabolism, elimination, and energy. For example, as Dr. Robert Scaer points out in *Trauma, Dissociation and Disease*, individuals who suffer from post-traumatic stress disorder are more susceptible to migraines, chronic pain, irritable bowel syndrome, and chronic fatigue. In addition, you may be so distracted by fear-induced stress that you bang into furniture, drive less skillfully, or burn yourself inadvertently. Since your immune system is already compromised, you may recover from such injuries less readily.

As you work with appreciation, even in a fear-inducing situation, you shift your perception and interpretation to what you can appreciate about the situation or its resolution. So if you do lose your job, instead of "How will I pay my bills?" being your first thought, with appreciation, it could be "I have a lot of valuable skills. I've gained experience and contacts on this job. I don't think it will be too long before I find another." You can feel your body relaxing from the initial shock of losing your job as you think these more appreciative thoughts. You are letting go of the fear that causes stress—and with it, damage to your bodily systems. As you continue in this mode, you nurture thoughts that value what you have to offer in the job market, and the opportunities available to you for productive job seeking. Your anxiety and stress levels continue to diminish. As a result, you handle problems more effectively. Your health and well-being benefit accordingly.

Adam, an AG member, notes that with appreciation, "Life is easier. I don't have that tight feeling of holding fear in my body so much anymore."

Appreciation supports good health by facilitating repair and renewal. Your body is constantly repairing and renewing itself, without your conscious awareness. The better your overall health and the lower your stress, the more easily and effortlessly this process occurs. Appreciation, by diminishing your stress levels, energizes your body, and facilitates this process.

Appreciating Your Way to Health: Losing Weight

Let's apply the five steps from chapter 5 to using appreciation in a health situation many of us deal with: losing weight.

Step One: Choose What You Want to Transform or Attract

You want to lose weight. That much is clear, but your desire is not specific enough. How much weight? If you answer, "I want to lose forty pounds," your next question should be, "And do I believe I can do that?" If the answer is "no," adjust the amount to something you can believe in. You can always choose a new goal once this first desire is fulfilled.

Give shape and form to your desire. Choosing to lose weight may not be sufficient for you to engage a powerful vibration. Being able to wear a smaller size, or taking ten inches off your waist may mean more to you. Again, give yourself a reality check: Do you really believe you can drop from a size 16 to a size 3? If so, great! Go for it. If not, adjust your choice to more accurately reflect what you think is possible.

Step Two: Determine the Feelings behind Your Desire

Discover the feelings behind your desire to lose weight by asking yourself, "Why do I want to lose weight?" Answering "Because I want to be thinner, duh!" is fine as long as it's accurate. But too often, "Why do I want to lose weight?" is more truthfully answered by, "Because my partner wants me to," or "Because I'm supposed to be thinner than I am."

The problem with answering the question in these ways, from a vibrational perspective, is that you are not 100 percent behind your desire. It isn't really what you want, so you'll lack the singular, intense focus necessary to successfully launch a vibration of appreciation for "weight loss." Make sure your desire to be more slender is something *you* want, for your own pleasure, for your own well-being.

Next, ask what the value of losing weight is to you. "I'll feel more attractive," you may say, or perhaps, "I'll feel better in my body. I'll have more energy," or

"I'll be able to bike with my friends," or "My health will improve." Think about that value; cherish the thought of feeling better, stronger, more attractive. Allow the accompanying sweet feelings of gratitude to well up inside of you. Let these good feelings flow through you and fill your mind and heart.

Step Three: Weed Out Conflicting Thoughts and Beliefs

Examine your beliefs regarding body size and weight. Weed out beliefs that conflict with your desire, and transform them. For example:

Current Belief	Changed Belief
Size shouldn't matter.	*My size matters to me. I'd like to change it, and it's OK for me to want that.*
Diets don't work for me.	*Diets work for some people; other approaches work for other people. I'll attract whatever approach I need to help me lose the weight I want to lose.*
Once you get big, you're fat forever.	*People change. I can start collecting success stories of people who've successfully lost weight and kept it off.*
No matter what I do, I can't lose weight.	*I haven't been successful in the past. That doesn't mean I won't be successful in the future.*

Once you've transformed the beliefs that stand in the way of a vibration of successfully losing weight, use affirmations to help you lock on to your new, more positive attitude, such as:

- The weight came on, the weight can come off.
- I'm good at attracting what I need.
- I can attract the perfect weight loss program for me.

Step Four: Launch Your Vibration of Appreciation

Before you can launch the vibration of appreciation for the more slender you, you must appreciate your current body shape and size. This is where many of us get stuck, because it's virtually impossible to look in the mirror at the pudgy mass clinging to your thighs and think, "I appreciate myself." It's beyond most of us to value and be grateful for ten pounds of cellulite! Fortunately, you don't have to appreciate cellulite in order to appreciate your thighs.

Switch your focus from what you hate about your thighs to what you can appreciate about them. For example, appreciate what willing servants your thighs are. Value how they carry you from place to place anytime you want. Be grateful that your thighs don't go on strike periodically and refuse to get you from chair to bed or take you up and down. Be grateful that your thighs provide wonderful support to the upper part of your body, with hardly a complaint. Value how healthy your thighs are, how beautifully the muscles, ligaments, and tendons work together, how little you have to think or worry about them. There is much to appreciate about a thigh, no matter how big or small!

Use this same approach for any body part, or your whole body. Value your body's health and strength. Be grateful for how beautifully it functions. Value the softness of your skin, be grateful for how marvelously it holds everything together! Thank your body for giving you the energy to go about your day. Be grateful for your body's willingness to sit, stand, eat, read, sing, hike, play— whatever you ask it to do. Get creative. Find as many things to appreciate about your body, "warts and all," as you can.

Pay attention to what you say to the mirror. Do you say, "Oh, I hate being so fat. I look awful," or "I wish I hadn't worn that, it makes me look huge"? Such thoughts reinforce a vibration of fat, not a vibration of slender. Switch your focus. Observe facets of your image that have nothing to do with fat or thin. Notice how a certain color complements your skin tone. Value your smile, appreciate the color of your eyes. Appreciate the cut of your hair, or how nice your nails look, or how well your accessories coordinate with your outfit. You can find many things about your image in a mirror to appreciate.

Now you're ready to launch the vibration of appreciation for your more slender you. Settle in a quiet place free of interruptions or distractions. Close your eyes, and start feeling appreciation for this wonderful desired shape. Think how you value this "new you," think of the ways in which being your new size will benefit you, be grateful for the wonderful feelings that will accompany your new weight. Focus single-mindedly and with great joy on how much you appreciate your desired shape. Don't allow conflicting thoughts or beliefs to interfere. Work your appreciation as vigorously and wholeheartedly as you can, and when you're done, relax and be happy. You've launched an exciting new vibration.

As you go about your life, stay clearly focused on your vibration of appreciation for the "new you," as well as your continuing appreciation for your current self. Clear out conflicting thoughts or feelings as they occur. In particular, look out for the natural tendency to compare yourself to others.

For example, you're walking down the street, doing a fine job appreciating yourself as you are, when you see Ms. Slenderella sashaying along, glued to the side of Mr. Gorgeous. You hate her reflexively, a pure gut reaction. You hate her for being slender without apparent effort, dressed in the latest you-have-to-be-a-size-three-to-wear-it diaphanous little nothing. In the same breath you hate yourself for not being all of the above. In the process, you're repelling the very vibration you seek, for you cannot hate someone who is slender and expect to vibrationally attract "slender."

What to do? Change how you perceive Ms. Slenderella and reinterpret her slimness. Appreciate her for being an example of "slender." When you next see her, think "Me—soon! Slender, wearing slender-people clothes—my turn next!" Value and be grateful to Ms. Slenderella for inspiring you. Remember the four-minute mile? It used to be thought a human impossibility. Then one athlete ran it, and since then, a number of other athletes have run it too. What seems impossible is indeed attainable. Transform your jealousy of anyone who has what you want by realizing that their accomplishments show you how available your desire really is.

Revisit your desired appreciation several times a week, to keep the vibration strong as it goes about its job of aligning and harmonizing with the thing you seek. A minute or so of vigorous appreciation should be enough to keep your vibration going.

Step Five: Work Your Appreciation

Trust that your vibration of appreciation for your chosen weight will align with a like vibration. Get ready to receive your desired weight. Look for all the ways in which you will attract your desired weight.

Dr. Seligman, in *Learned Optimism*, says of optimists that the word in their heart is "yes," as opposed to pessimists, whose word in their heart is "no." So it is with appreciators. Let the word in your heart be a resounding "Yes!" for you never know how your desire will be attracted to you. You may hear of a book extolling a new diet that appeals to you. A girlfriend may invite you to a spinning class, something you've never tried. Before you say "No," think "Maybe this is my desire starting to come," and say "Yes! I've never done it before but I'm willing to try."

You may read an article or see a news item on a health program about how Pilates, a method of mental and physical conditioning, facilitates weight loss. You may just not feel as hungry as before. You may find yourself wanting only certain foods, and not interested in others. You may discover gardening, and shed pounds as you weed and fertilize. You may get excited over a new project and find that eating holds much less interest. You may fall in love with an athletically inclined person and discover that bicycling is tremendous fun.

Be alert to all the ways your desired weight or size may be attracted into your life. Appreciate whatever comes your way, believing that all things can contribute to the unfolding of your desire.

Bear in mind that you still have to take action! Although vibration will attract like vibration, you must follow the leads and impulses you receive, for those are the promptings of your vibration. Of course, keep on exercising your good common judgement; not feeling as hungry as before doesn't mean that you don't eat for three days! Discovering the joys of spinning class doesn't mean that you spin three hours a day, seven days a week.

Appreciation is one approach to health and healing. It is meant to align your vibration with all that vibrates towards health and healing, not to replace other treatments or methodologies that are also of use to you.

Whether appreciating yourself, others, the world around you, or life itself, appreciation can contribute greatly to your body's wellness, and to the greater enjoyment of life such wellness leads to. Make appreciation part of what Dr. Pert calls your "daily, emotional self care."

As one wise seventy-nine-year-old AG member noted, when asked how he was doing: "Fine. I'm always fine. Some days I'm just more fine than others."

Not only does this man's appreciative attitude contribute to his "feeling fine," it contributes to his experience of *positive* aging, one of the most exciting benefits appreciation can bring to your life, as you'll see in the next chapter.

10

Appreciate Your Way to Positive Aging

Aging is inevitable. How we age, however, is far from predetermined. In this chapter we'll show you how to use the power of appreciation to transform aging into a positive, happy experience. After all, what good is long life without happiness?

To experience aging in a positive way is an individual decision, not something you can take for granted. Our society, focused on youth, physical beauty, and the ability to produce, fails to value the characteristics and qualities that emerge in later life—when beauty is more internal, and productivity is of the mind and soul rather than of material goods or services.

Ironically, even as society fails to value later life, we are living longer. According to the National Institute of Health's 2001 figures, people over sixty-five were 4 percent of the United States population in 1900, 13 percent in the year 2000, and will constitute fully *20 percent of our population* by the year 2025! According to the U.S. Census Bureau, the population sixty-five and over increased 1000 percent from 1900 to 2000—from 3.1 million to 35 million—compared to a 350 percent increase for the total population. The growth of the population eighty-five and over increased from 122,000 in 1900 to 4.2 million in 2000. The number of centenarians more than doubled between 1980 and 1990, and these numbers continue to rise.

Enter appreciation, which recognizes and supports worth. Regardless of society's values, you can choose to appreciate the worth of the people who are aging around you and the older self you are becoming. The older you is no less precious and wonderful than the younger you! You are simply different.

In the August 2002 issue of the *Journal of Personality and Social Psychology*, Dr. Becca R. Levy and other researchers at Yale University reported that adults who had positive attitudes and self-perceptions about aging lived more than seven years longer than same-age adults who had negative attitudes and self-perceptions. The researchers noted that "self-perceptions of aging had a greater impact on survival than did gender, socioeconomic status, loneliness and functional health," and that the impact of positive self-perceptions had greater effect on longevity than lowered blood pressure, lower cholesterol levels, exercise, weight loss, or nonsmoking (all of which, in and of themselves, add years to one's life).

Studies have shown that a common trait among centenarians is a great appreciation for the simple experiences and pleasures of life. More specifically, Dr. Stephen P. Jewett's extensive New York study of the psychological characteristics of centenarians showed that they share certain traits: optimism, a distinct sense of humor, an enjoyment of life, an ability to see beauty where others would see ugliness, and an appreciation for the simple pleasures of life and satisfaction in day-to-day living.

Betty, seventy-two and an AG member, notes, "I can see a direct result every time I'm appreciating. My overall energy feels good. I feel more integrated and more comfortable with what I'm doing and why."

In the famous "Nun Study" conducted by Deborah D. Danner and David A. Snowdon, along with Wallace V. Friesen and researchers at the College of Medicine at the University of Kentucky, handwritten autobiographies from 180 Catholic nuns, written for the most part when the nuns were in their early twenties, were analyzed for their emotional content. The results were then compared to the nuns' survival between the ages of seventy-five and ninety-five. The study showed that nuns who articulated more positive emotions—such as feelings of accomplishment, amusement, contentment, gratitude, happiness, hope, interest, love, and relief—in their early-life autobiographies lived as much as ten years longer than those expressing fewer positive emotions. Snowdon stated that his findings went along with "other studies that have shown that people who rated more positive on personality tests were more likely to live longer than those who were more pessimistic . . . It feels good to be happy and hopeful. It's an enjoyable state that produces very little stress, and the body thrives in those conditions." Thus the natural consequence—longevity.

Appreciating aging requires a radical change in perspective. If all you see in the aging process is decrepitude and decline, you're unlikely to look forward to your later years. Many people view aging as a slow progression towards death, completely ignoring the fact that death comes at all ages, not reserving itself for old age. The first step in appreciating aging, therefore, is to redefine it as one of the stages of life. When you think of aging as the *living* you do in your seventies, eighties, nineties, and hundreds, suddenly aging takes on a different value. The emphasis has shifted from "declining towards death," an experience difficult (at best) to appreciate, to "living life," a much easier experience to appreciate.

Ninety-two-year-old Mary Ruth Brasfield of Wichita, Kansas, as described by Marie Snider in her Kansan Online article, "This Side of 60," is the antithesis of a senior "declining towards death." When Mary Ruth was seventy, her daughter,

Barbara Hoffmann, asked her mom if she could help in Barbara's tropical plant business, "Tropical Design." Mary Ruth's response was, "I have plastic plants and I'm totally happy with them," but she began working in the business, and found the "love of her life" in tropical plants. To this day, Mary Ruth is a key player in the business: she is the buyer and bill payer, a job she loves so much that she doesn't hesitate to take work home and often works until midnight. Mary Ruth loves her life. Her daughter Barbara says, "She's ninety-two, but she's young. She works all the time. I've lived my life just trying to keep up."

Bust Your Preconceptions of Aging

Appreciating aging requires busting some misconceptions. Too many of us think of aging as withering away, lonely, incompetent, and infirm, left to die in a nursing home, out of sight and out of mind. No wonder we don't look forward with joy to aging! In fact, only 4.5 percent (1.56 million) of the population sixty-five and over lived in nursing homes in 2000, according to the U.S. Census Bureau.

Unfortunately, our perception of aging is skewed by this small percentage. Since we don't see many older people around us in our everyday lives, we reason erroneously that if they're not in the workplace or at the mall, they must be in nursing homes. Even physicians, because they are used to seeing older people sick, not well, tend to assume that most older people are sick—in reality they are simply seeing the few sick individuals within a much larger, healthy, aging population.

Begin your appreciation of later life by challenging your preconceptions about aging. Observe older people who are enjoying their lives. There are plenty of them—and plenty of famous ones to read about. Explore what these people have to say about the value of being older. Many people have spoken, for example, of the freedom from social constraints that comes with age. Older people often feel that their many years entitle them to speak their minds without reservation, and to dress, eat, and behave how they please. Agnes, a spry AG member, comments, with a twinkle in her eye, "I'm eighty-one years young. I married my seventy-seven-year-old husband this year—and oh the stink my kids and grandkids put up about it. He was a bachelor, so he didn't have any family to squawk, lucky man. Well, I told my family I'd lived my whole life trying to please this one and that one, and I was done with that, thank you very much. I told them they should be happy we weren't living in sin! Which of course we had been, but I didn't see any need to rub their noses in it. I am still a lady, after all."

Appreciate the benefits aging brings to you and to others, such as life-review and the making of amends. As James Hillman says in *The Force of Character*, the "cosmological speculation and confabulation of memories into stories" is the enduring stuff of our personal myths, which connects us with our ancestors and leads to a deepening of the soul, spirituality, and all that is mystical.

Aging is an extremely personal thing. Some people never experience certain symptoms of aging, others experience them long before the average age of onset. The mistake many people make after the age of forty-five or so is to assume that any ache or pain, any change in function, is an irreversible consequence of aging. When you're twenty-five and you have indigestion, you pop an antacid and go about your day. When you're sixty-five and have indigestion, you may think, "Oh my God, gastric distress, I'm getting older, I can't digest my food any longer. I wonder if I've got colon cancer." When you feel tired after a long day, at thirty-five you think "Gotta get to bed earlier tonight"; at sixty-five, you think "I'm getting old, I can't keep going the way I used to." Frequently, however, what you assume to be a function of aging is just the result of the simple fact that "what you don't use, you lose." As ninety-three-year-old Buddy Ebsen (who played Jed Clampett in *The Beverly Hillbillies* TV series) told Scott Walter of

Parade Magazine, he's up by 7:00 A.M. every day, exercises before breakfast, and then writes or paints the rest of the day. He's currently writing his fourth book, a mystery. Ebsen says: "I have a motto in Latin over my door that proclaims, 'Use it or lose it.'" Apparently Ebsen is in no mood to lose it!

Even if you haven't "used it" in a while, you haven't lost it irretrievably. As Deepak Chopra noted in *Ageless Body, Timeless Mind*, even the "fragile" elderly are stronger, with more regenerative powers, than we think:

> Daring gerontologists at Tufts University visited a nursing home, selected a group of the frailest residents, and put them on a weight-training regimen. One might fear that a sudden introduction to exercise would exhaust or kill these fragile people, but in fact they thrived. Within eight weeks, wasted muscles had come back by 300 percent, coordination and balance improved, and overall a sense of active life returned. Some of the subjects who had not been able to walk unaided could now get up and go to the bathroom in the middle of the night by themselves, an act of reclaimed dignity that is by no means trivial. What makes this accomplishment truly wondrous, however, is that the youngest subject in the group was eighty-seven, and the oldest ninety-six.

Not using some part of ourselves often comes from a change in *perception*. If you have an underlying belief that old people are fragile, you will fail to appreciate your own resilient musculature, and "use it" less and less. You will perceive fatigue as proof that you're too old to exert yourself, instead of perceiving it as your body's way of saying, "Hey, let's try different ways of exercising." When you appreciate that your body will be able to sustain movement and muscular effort, you look for ways to be physically active, rather than relegating "being physical" to the young.

Categorizing your weaknesses and imperfections as a consequence of aging limits your ability to deal creatively and effectively with them. When you're twenty-five, and you forget your phone number momentarily, you think "Wow, I must really be distracted"; when you're fifty-five you think, "Oh, no, I'm getting Alzheimer's." You focus and dwell on the possible horrors ahead, rather than simply doing what you'd have done at twenty-five, and saying "Dang, I'd better write things down," and being done with it. This is not to say that there aren't medical conditions that require professional help, just that there is no need to attach "and it's because I'm old" to every condition.

Instead of labeling yourself as "old," look at your changing body as simply functioning differently. Appreciate your ability to compensate for that difference, just as the differently abled do. You will then start *living* your later years rather than submitting to them.

Dottie, an eighty-three-year-old AG member whose Southern accent gives away her Tennessee roots, says:

You know, I don't think of myself as having limitations—although of course I do. Let's see: there's my balance, it's terrible, and if I don't use my walker I fall down a lot. Then there's my energy—I get tired much more easily than I used to. I don't have much strength in my hands. And of course my arthritis kicks up regularly. But you know, I have all of my mind, except for my memory and that's what notepads are for. My eyesight is great and I only need glasses to read. My hearing is good. I can still take care of myself even if I am awfully slow. So I have a cane and a walker, and depending on the day, I use one or the other.

I think of myself as "grandma longlegs" which is what my grandson calls me, and I am oh-so-grateful I can get around on my own. I don't think about my "limitations" much because they don't feel that way to me. For example, there always seems to be some nice person around to help me get things off the shelf in the supermarket or whenever I can't grab ahold of something or lift it. I two-finger peck on the computer and I can surf the Web with the best of them. There's a whole group of us that chat every day on the Internet, visiting and catching up on news, sending each other jokes and pictures and all the rest of it.

I take little naps at odd times during the day when I feel tired. I think of them as my "beauty naps." I have a game with the weatherman as to who predicts the weather better: him or my arthritis. It's hard to travel, so I travel through books and television; that Discovery channel is something. I conduct orchestras sitting in my easy chair listening to music with my eyes closed. I nurse a little herb garden on my kitchen window sill because I can't kneel down in the dirt to help a regular garden grow. I listen to books on tape when my eyes get tired of reading, and let the voices take me to other people's lives and experiences. I sit with my grandchildren and tell them tall tales of days gone by. I do all the relaxing things I never had time for when I was raising my family and taking care of my husband and working.

Yes, my life is different—but life is different every step along the way. I feel so blessed and fortunate to have the life I've got. Limitations? Frankly, my dear, to steal a famous line, I don't give a damn. Life is good and I'm enjoying it any way I can.

Appreciation can change your perception of more than your physical self in your later years, it can also change your perception of who you are. Because society devalues older people, they tend to devalue themselves. Giving people a sense of value almost miraculously rejuvenates them, as shown by a classic 1988 study conducted by Harvard psychologist Ellen Langer and colleagues. In the experiment, a group of healthy men, seventy-five or older, spent a week at a retreat. The retreat was decorated in keeping with the styles, reading materials, and music of 1959, the year in which the men would have been in their mid-forties and mid-fifties. The men were not allowed to talk about anything that had happened since 1959, and were to talk in the present tense about their families, careers, and lives as if it were actually 1959. They were given photo identification of themselves at their 1959 ages, and learned to refer to each other by looking at those pictures. The men were treated as if they had the intelligence and independence of younger men, and given complex instructions to follow about their daily routine, even though in their regular lives many were dependent on younger family members to perform daily tasks for them. The men were asked their opinions on various matters in a respectful way, and those opinions were actually listened to, something that almost never happened in their regular lives. In other words, the men were valued. Their ability and intelligence were appreciated in the same way they had been when they were twenty years younger.

In her book, *Mindfulness*, Langer writes of the amazing results of her study: impartial judges who examined photographs of the men before and after the retreat observed that the men looked visibly younger by an average of three years. People's fingers tend to shorten with age, yet the men's fingers were found to have lengthened after this brief experiment. Their joints became more flexible. Their posture began to straighten, resembling more their posture when they were younger. Their muscle strength improved, as did their hearing and vision. Not only that, but over half of the "1959ers" scored higher on IQ tests after the retreat, even though intelligence is usually considered to be unchangeable once you're an adult.

Because being "old" is equated in our society with incompetence, if you're not vigorously appreciating yourself, you are tacitly accepting society's definition of you. Society expects you to be dull, boring, a useless burden that will be tolerated at best, shunned at worst. Yet, as Langer's and other studies prove, when you refuse society's definition and stubbornly value your older self, behaving in ways that reflect that valuing, you become interested and interesting, curious, alert, capable of far more physically, mentally, and emotionally than expected. You don't even conform to gerontologists' expectations of shortening fingers and wasting muscles! You become who you really are: a unique and vibrant individual, rich in experience and qualities, fully capable of participating in life in a myriad of ways.

Value yourself by appreciating who you are, not who you aren't; what you can be and do, rather than what you can't. You may find, much to your surprise, that the wisdom borne of your years of experience counts for more than the agility and strength of your youth. The wisdom of experience can actually save your life, as described by Deepak Chopra in *Ageless Body, Timeless Mind*:

> In the sea battles of World War I, German sailors were sometimes stranded for days or weeks after their ships were sunk. Invariably, the first men to die were the youngest. This phenomenon remained a mystery until it was realized that the older sailors, who had survived earlier sinkings, knew that the crisis could be weathered; lacking such experience, the young sailors perished because they saw themselves as trapped in a hopeless situation.

As you age, notice and value your compassion, your caring, your sense of humor, your tenaciousness, your strong opinions. Appreciate your memory, whatever shape it is in—for the more you appreciate what is, the more of that you will attract. Appreciate the creative way that you get around any physical inconveniences. Appreciate the parts of your body that work magnificently, and how valiantly the imperfect parts of you do the best that they can. Greet yourself with appreciation when you catch a glimpse of yourself in a mirror. Appreciate your smile, the twinkle in your eye, the marvelous expressiveness of your brow. "I know it sounds silly," Helen (a buxom seventy-eight-year-old widow and AG member) says, "but every time I look at myself in the mirror before brushing my teeth in the morning, I say 'Hello there, you great big beautiful doll,' because that's what my husband used to call me, and it makes me feel good. Even if I wake up achy or full of cricks, and the day doesn't feel like it's off to a good start, I still say it, and somehow things don't seem all that bad."

Be aware of internal mutterings, for what you think and feel influences your body's ability to heal and rejuvenate. For example, when you say "I'm too old," your beliefs, thoughts, and feelings about being "old" convey chemical messages to your cells, which faithfully respond by behaving according to those beliefs. If instead of saying "I'm too old," you say "I'm too tired," your cells will respond according to your beliefs about being tired, which hopefully includes the belief that a good night's rest will restore you.

As has often been said, "You don't stop growing when you get old. You get old when you stop growing." Appreciating life will keep you vibrant and curious, and will nurture you. Appreciating life will keep you truly alive, as opposed to merely existing. Paul, a seventy-two-year-old retired mechanic and AG member, noted that with his new appreciation of his older self, "I feel in control, in the good sense of the word, of my future and the way it will unfold. I know I'm doing all that I can for myself—and that makes everything else OK."

Staying focused in the present, looking forward to a positive future, and being open to change and willing to learn are vital ingredients to happiness in later life. When you deliberately look for ways to appreciate your life, right here and now, you stay firmly rooted in the present, and are more accepting of the changes that the present may require.

Appreciating your present does not mean diminishing your past. However, focusing exclusively on your past imprisons you in yesterday's ways of doing and being. Appreciating the benefits of your past, as well as the possibilities inherent in your present, expands your ways of doing and being.

When you believe that the life available to older people is dull, boring, and devoid of passion, you will approach your future with dread and foreboding. When you appreciate, you are more willing to go towards that future with curiosity and eager anticipation.

Beliefs That Help, Beliefs That Hinder

Certain beliefs can stand in the way of your continued growth and exploration of life. Examine your beliefs: if, for example, you hold to "You can't teach an old dog new tricks," you confine yourself to repeating your past. This is not a belief that supports movement into an expanded present or future. "You're never too old to learn," on the other hand, is an empowering belief that keeps you pointed firmly towards growth.

Believing that certain activities or behaviors are not appropriate for older persons will limit your exploration of life. Believing that any activity or behavior that does not endanger yourself or another is appropriate regardless of age opens up all sorts of possibilities.

Gladys, a vigorous eighty-two-year-old AG member, tells us:

I'm from England originally. We came over because of WWII, and I spent most of my life raising my family. I had three boys and they were the usual handful. As each of my sons married, the grandbabies came along and that kept me plenty busy. After my husband retired, life was mostly about family, golf, and a little traveling—mostly to play golf—but always together. We did everything together, my husband and I.

Well, after my husband passed away twelve years ago, I was at loose ends. I felt myself growing old overnight, sitting in the house all by myself. Finally one day I shook myself and said "Enough!" If God hadn't taken me, then I wasn't dead yet and should stop acting like I was. I started asking 'round and found there were part time administrative and clerical positions open at our sheriff's department. This intrigued me, and even though I'd never worked outside the home, and certainly never thought of myself as a "police" type, I thought I'd try it.

The sheriff took one look at me and said, "Are you sure you're up to this?"

I said, "I don't know, but I'd like to give it a try."

He laughed and said I had the right attitude, and after we'd talked a while and he had me fill out some papers and take a test, he said the job was mine if I wanted it, and that I had a three-month probation period to see if it worked out.

Well, my dear, my world just opened up. I answered telephone calls and filed papers, that sort of thing, nothing all that complicated and yet I was thrilled. I felt young again! I was busy, I felt needed, and the young men and women were all so nice to me. I made it through my probation period, and lucky me, I've been there ever since. After three years in a clerical position, they moved me into an administrative position where I actually get to work on reports and all sorts of interesting case matters.

You should see the look on people's faces when I tell them I work for the sheriff's department! What a wonderful experience this has been. My only regret is that my dear departed Brian isn't here to share it with me—although I do tell him all the goings-on fairly regularly.

One of the most delightful fruits of later years is the desire to appreciate others. Free from the cares of daily responsibility, grandparents cherish their grandchildren, and are often amazed and delighted at their antics, the same antics that might have seemed unremarkable or annoying to them when they were raising children themselves. One grandmother states, "When my two-year-old grandson splashes water all over the place in the bath, I find myself laughing with him and marveling at the spontaneity of his expression."

Appreciation of others is often also expressed by volunteering, which contributes significantly to the life-satisfaction and well-being of those who volunteer. It's a win-win situation, for even as you appreciate those you give to, they are appreciating you and what you have to offer. When you volunteer, you are productive, you feel valuable and valued, your self-esteem rises accordingly, and you avoid seeing yourself as a victim. You connect with others and avoid the all-too-common pitfall of aging: isolation. You don't allow society's definition of your life as boring and impoverished to rule how you go about your life.

Luke, a seventy-five-year-old appreciator, says:

I've worked all of my life, from the time I was about sixteen, bussing tables at a diner, until I retired from my job of managing a warehouse for a citrus grower, that I'd had for close to thirty years. I'm divorced from way back and never did have any kids, so I found myself with an awful lot of time on my hands. I'd always thought I'd use those "golden years" to go fishing or bowling or something like that, and spend time with the guys, but my body was too beat up from all those years of hauling crates and driving forklifts and all the rest of it, and my buddies are retiring down to Florida or elsewhere with their wives.

I was getting pretty darn bored and not knowing what to do with myself when I walked into the library one day and saw some lady reading to a bunch of kids. They looked like they were having a lot of fun. They were real cute little tykes, and the librarian must have seen the look on my face, because she said: "We could always use another helping hand."

I thought, what do I know about books? Nothing. But the librarian said it's just children's books, and they're happy as long as someone is reading to them, and that the library really needed more readers. I thought, OK, I'll give it a shot, so I did.

Well darned if I didn't have the best time doing it. I was kind of nervous at first, and I stumbled over my words, but the kids didn't seem to mind, and after a while I got pretty good at it. It became a regular thing. I'd read to the kids three times a week, just for a half hour—that's about all they can pay attention to, and I found that half hour was the highlight of my day. I started thinking up funny ways to tell the stories, and I bought a hand puppet for one of the stories, which really cracked the kids up.

Then the librarian got me going on this other thing. I help young people learn to read better, a couple of hours a week. It's a good thing I don't have to help them read anything complicated, because I never made it past the tenth grade, but that doesn't seem to matter. If I don't know what a word means, we just look it up together.

I gotta tell you, I look at this volunteering thing as doing more for me than it does for the kids! Do I appreciate it? You bet. It surely does put a smile on my face.

Helen, an AG member, who at sixty-eight volunteers three afternoons a week at the information desk at a hospital, says, "I not only enjoy others more since I've been volunteering, but I enjoy myself more, and so my family enjoys me more. I hope appreciation will always be a tool I remember to use on a daily basis."

When you make appreciation the lens through which you view life, make it your habitual state of mind, aging ceases to be a frightening experience. You are better able to deal with whatever changes come, and to make your later years a truly positive experience.

11

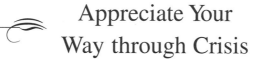

Appreciate Your
Way through Crisis

The love of your life deserts you for another. The promotion that you've been putting in hours of unpaid overtime to land goes to the assistant you trained. The funny skin thing on your face is melanoma. You're downsized out of your dream job. Your child is rendered a quadriplegic by a drunk driver. You are diagnosed with terminal cancer. Your life savings are squandered by a corrupt money manager. Your husband is killed in a factory fire.

Traumatic to varying degrees, these are all crises: times when life changes abruptly, when its predictable routine is suddenly and swiftly interrupted and the future looks uncertain if not bleak. All of us are faced with crises sooner or later, and have to deal with them.

Using appreciation as a transformative tool in the face of crisis may seem ludicrous. What is there to appreciate in the death of a loved one? In a child's injury? In losing the job of your dreams? On the surface, nothing at all. Yet when you examine the nature of crisis more closely, you realize that appreciation can indeed play a critical role.

The Dual Nature of Crisis

Crisis holds within it both light and dark aspects; folk wisdom recognizes that "every cloud has a silver lining." The Chinese word for crisis expresses this duality particularly clearly; it is composed of two characters: "wei" meaning "danger," and "chi" meaning "opportunity." Danger is the cloud and opportunity is the silver lining.

The danger lies in losing ourselves in the crisis, letting it overwhelm and destroy us. The opportunity lies in the discovery of new or latent qualities within, the revelation of new possibilities, dreams, and desires never before considered or even imagined, our rising phoenix-like, stronger and eventually happier than ever.

What is appreciation's role in all this? Appreciation can help you see your way through the storm of emotions that crisis brings with it. It can shake you loose from being immobilized by grief, and it can help you build a bridge from the danger to the opportunity.

Appreciation Lifts You out of Mental and Emotional Chaos

How do you feel when you experience a crisis? Shock, panic, fear, anger, rage, depression, despair, anxiety, confusion, dread, and horror—these emotions that may accompany crisis can lead to chaos in your heart and mind, an inability to focus or to see your way through. Appreciation can soothe you, by bringing order to your cataclysmic thoughts and feelings, and allowing you to see possibilities.

Your brain constantly sends messages through your autonomic nervous system—that part of the nervous system that controls and regulates internal organs, without any conscious recognition or effort. In a state of crisis, your heart rate is jerky, random, and incoherent. Your heart activity generates signals that travel back to the brain and influence what you perceive, how you think and make decisions, and how you feel. A chaotic heart rate is reflected in chaotic thoughts; you are unable to focus clearly and think productively.

Appreciation can literally lift you out of mental and emotional chaos. Find something, even something small, to appreciate in the moment of crisis, and you can calm yourself and restore your mental clarity. When you are in a place of great negative emotion, your range of thought and feeling is extremely limited. You cannot see beyond your fear, anger, or despair. Appreciation returns you to the fullness of yourself. As you appreciate, you reconnect with a broader range of thought and feeling, and can see possibilities beyond the immediacy of your distress. Juan, a twenty-seven-year-old AG member, had this to say:

When my brother was murdered, I was enraged. I remember bellowing to the skies how unfair it was, and how could God let this happen? My brother was only thirty-five years old. He was gunned down in a botched bank robbery. He was just standing in line, like everybody else, waiting for the teller. I was a mess, screaming, crying, hollering — no good to anyone.

Then a neighbor said to me, "He was a good man, your brother. He led a good life," and that pulled me up short. I started thinking about all the good things my brother was, and how much fun we'd had together. I realized I could appreciate who he'd been and how much he'd given to me and to our families while he was alive, instead of railing at his death.

It kind of calmed me down. I was still sad and unhappy, but at least I wasn't raging all the time. And I found that as I got calm, I was able to help my brother's wife with everything you need to do when someone gets killed that way. We started sharing stories about my brother, her husband, talking about what we appreciated about him, and somehow that helped my sister-in-law with her grief. It made me feel better to help her, and then I looked around and found ways to help out with my nieces and nephew.

I can't say appreciation made me outright happy, but it sure made it easier to move through my feelings and get to a place where I could be of use to someone.

When faced with a crisis, your emotions are the first thing you must deal with. You can't think clearly in the midst of powerful negative emotions. You certainly can't appreciate before those emotions have been expressed. The danger lies not in expressing your emotions, but in dwelling on them. Acknowledge painful emotions. Don't pretend that they don't exist in order to get to appreciation faster—it won't work.

For example, if you've just been diagnosed with cancer, allow yourself to feel shock or fear. Allow the emotions to flow through you, expressing them in ways that seem appropriate and safe to you. Then, as soon as you can, instead of returning to the thoughts accompanying those emotions, running them through your head over and over, thereby amplifying them, ask yourself, "OK, what can I value here? What can I be grateful for?" Your first appreciative thought might be something as basic as "I'm still alive right now. I can appreciate that. Where there's life, there's hope. OK. I can appreciate that."

Almost immediately, your fear and panic will begin to subside, as long as you don't return to your earlier thoughts. Remember that your thoughts are within your control! Stick with appreciative thoughts as much as you can. From there, you will be able to see a slightly larger range of possibilities: "I have a good doctor. I can appreciate that. And there are other doctors. They've done a lot of research on cancer. My cousin had cancer and she got through it. I can appreciate that. I'm not alone here; I can appreciate that."

Little by little, one appreciative thought at a time, you can appreciate your way out of the fear and panic into a more productive way of thinking and feeling. As you shift into appreciative thoughts and feelings, your heart and brain synchronize, your entire electromagnetic field becomes harmonious, and you attract experiences in line with those vibrations.

At times, emotions will well up spontaneously. When they do, allow them to flow, express them appropriately and safely, and then strive to switch your focus to an appreciative thought. Be genuine. To say "I appreciate this cancer" when you're in the midst of the pain of chemotherapy would be a lie. You may never appreciate the cancer. That's not necessary. You can appreciate the researchers who developed the chemotherapy that has saved so many, as it may very well save you. You can appreciate how valiantly and determinedly your body is absorbing the chemo and using it to your benefit. You can appreciate the support of your friends and family.

Don't overreach. Don't say, "And I appreciate everything all these wonderful doctors and nurses are doing for me," if you think the nurses are too rough with you, and you hate most of the treatment. The vibration you emit will be soured by the untruthful portions of your experience. Instead, stick with what is specifically true, to preserve the integrity of your vibration of appreciation. If all you can appreciate is the hope that maybe the chemo is working, then focus on that. If that's your truth, that's what you put out there. Vibration is never fooled.

Appreciate Your Way through the Paralysis of Being Overwhelmed

Crisis tends to overwhelm. Too much happens too fast, or you feel threatened by something too powerful or too unknown to cope with. When you're overwhelmed, you feel powerless and you freeze up. Fear, shock, or despair take over. You don't move, you don't act, you don't respond effectively. When you're overwhelmed, your focus is narrow in the extreme; all you can see is complete disaster.

Appreciation can free you of this paralyzing immobility by empowering you to respond, thereby lifting you out of helplessness. Appreciation throws a switch, letting you travel from powerless to powerful in the space of a thought. The moment you find something of value in yourself or a situation, you liberate yourself from being overwhelmed. You can see alternatives other than disaster, so you can take action. Your ability to function has been restored.

Jen, an AG member, finds that crisis "just throws me off and knocks me out of that place where I want to be. Appreciating brings me back to that place; it is something I need to go back to and stay strong with."

Peter Levine, in *Waking the Tiger: Healing Trauma*, tells a story that reveals the lifesaving power of appreciation. In 1976, twenty-six children were kidnapped from their school bus outside Chowchilla, California. The children, aged five to fifteen years, were imprisoned inside two dark vans in an underground vault for approximately thirty hours. They escaped and were treated for physical injuries at a local hospital, but received no psychiatric care. No one seemed to think they needed it, even an expert consulted at the time stated that he believed only one of the twenty-six might be affected. This was in line with the psychiatric beliefs of the day.

Eight months later, the children were studied by Dr. Lenore Terr, also a psychiatrist. Dr. Terr found quite the opposite effect—that the event had had severe long-term psychological, medical, and social impact on nearly all of the children. The one exception was a fourteen-year-old, Bob Barklay, who was considerably less severely affected.

Bob was the boy who, when the pole supporting the roof gave way and the ceiling began to collapse on the children, responded by looking actively for a way out; enlisting the help of another boy, he dug a tunnel through which all the children escaped.

Bob, in other words, looked for what could be of value in the situation, what he could appreciate, and used it. The other children were caught in the dread of their imminent death, unable to see anything else. They were so overwhelmed that they had to be urged through the tunnel to freedom.

Not only did Bob's appreciation of what could be lifesaving in the situation literally save the children's lives, it also preserved his own mental and emotional well-being by restoring him to a sense of personal effectiveness.

Appreciation helps you break free of immobility by focusing your attention on what you have, rather than what you do not; what you are, rather than what you are not; what you can do, rather than on what you cannot. Appreciating what *is* helps you see the many ways in which you are *not* a victim, helpless and hopeless. Focusing on what *isn't* reinforces all the ways in which you *are* a victim.

Recognizing and appreciating our own power, and changing our perspective from what we can't do to what we can, transforms our ability to respond to a fearful situation. In the weeks following September 11, 2001, Americans feared another assault. Air passengers were especially prone to anxiety, dreading a fatal replay. Peter Hannaford, a passenger aboard a United Airlines flight, described in a *Washington Times* article how one man's words provided the catalyst that awakened air passengers to appreciate the considerable powers they possessed to protect their own safety:

As it was at most U.S. airports, last Saturday was the first near normal day at Denver International since the terrorist attacks. On United's Flight 564 the door had just been locked and the plane was about to pull out of the gate when the captain came on the public address system.

"I want to thank you brave folks for coming out today. We don't have any new instructions from the federal government, so from now on we're on our own."

The passengers listened in total silence. He explained that airport security measures had pretty much solved the problem of firearms being carried aboard, but not weapons of the type the terrorists apparently used, plastic knives or those fashioned from wood or ceramics.

"Sometimes a potential hijacker will announce that he has a bomb. There are no bombs on this aircraft and if someone were to get up and make that claim, don't believe him. If someone were to stand up, brandish something such as a plastic knife and say 'This is a hijacking' or words to that effect here is what you should do: Every one of you should stand up and immediately throw things at that person—pillows, books, magazines, eyeglasses, shoes—anything that will throw him off balance and distract his attention. If he has a confederate or two, do the same with them. Most important: get a blanket over him, then wrestle him to floor and keep him there. We'll land the plane at the nearest airport and the authorities will take it from there.

"Remember, there will be one of him and maybe a few confederates, but there are two hundred of you. You can overwhelm them.

"The Declaration of Independence says 'We, the people' and that's just what it is when we're up in the air: we, the people, vs. would-be terrorists. I don't think we are going to have any such problem today or tomorrow or for a while, but sometime down the road, it is going to happen again and I want you to know what to do.

"Now, since we're a family for the next few hours, I'll ask you to turn to the person next to you, introduce yourself, tell them a little about yourself and ask them to do the same."

The end of this remarkable speech brought sustained clapping from the passengers. He had put the matter in perspective.

More than that, the pilot had *empowered* the passengers. Although he never used the word "appreciate," he was encouraging his passengers to do just that: to value and be grateful for what was available to them in the event of an attack (weapons of defense in the form of books, magazines, shoes, their strength in numbers), rather than dwelling on what wasn't available to them (a complete feeling of safety).

Switching your focus to what you can appreciate in any given situation, rather than what is no longer available to you, is critical to freeing yourself of the immobility of being overwhelmed, and to helping you build to the opportunity within crisis.

Building the Bridge from Danger to Opportunity

After you use appreciation to help you through the emotional storm and overwhelming experience of crisis, use it to build a bridge from the events at hand—be they minor or major crises—to solutions, possibilities, and opportunities.

For example, let's say you step into a mud puddle and splatter your clothes as you're rushing to an important appointment—a small crisis. Your first thought may be, "Oh, no! My clothes are ruined! I'm going to make a poor impression, and I'll never make this sale." Instead, use appreciation to build towards your desired positive outcome: "OK, my clothes are a mess, but I'm not hurt and my mind is intact. I can appreciate that." From this awareness, you can go one step further: you can appreciate that everyone has stepped in a mud puddle or had a similar mishap on the way to a meeting. The folks you are going to see will empathize and not judge you on the basis of the stains on your clothes, but on your skills and talents. They may even admire the aplomb you show in the face of adversity. Now you're ready to use appreciation to actually create opportunity for yourself!

In your appreciative state of mind, as you stand there, shaking mud off your freshly polished shoes, you ask yourself, "What is of value here? What can I find or create to appreciate?" You may decide to use yourself in your presentation as a living example of how the service or product you sell would benefit someone in just such a situation. You may remember and value your still-intact sense of humor, and come up with a funny anecdote for your prospective client, thereby making him more receptive. There is opportunity even in mud puddles! Appreciation can help you find it.

Mud puddles are a minor crisis; paralysis is not. Many of us would regard becoming a paraplegic at age eighteen, confined to a wheelchair, as a life sentence of despair. Not Ralf Hotchkiss, as described by Noelle Nelson in *Winner Takes All*. Ralf truly appreciates his situation, the result of a motorcycle accident. He considers himself to have been liberated by his wheelchair.

Now in his fifties, Ralf has devoted his life to designing and building wheelchairs. His company, the Whirlwind Network, collaborates with thirty-three wheelchair makers in twenty-five countries, sharing innovations towards a continually better and more liberating wheelchair. After his accident, Ralf looked for and found within his paralysis the opportunity to benefit himself and a lot of other people. By appreciating what he could do, and what actually served him from the motorcycle accident, he systematically built the bridge from crisis to opportunity, and to the positive future he now enjoys.

Appreciation can help you create opportunity even in the face of death. In another example from Nelson's *Winner Takes All*, Myrtle Faye Rumph lost her only son, Al Wooten, Jr., then thirty-five years old, in a drive-by shooting. Relatives clamored for revenge, but Myrtle saw opportunity in the crisis. Rather than avenge her son's death, she chose to honor him by valuing and being grateful for what makes children grow up in safety. She created the Al Wooten, Jr. Heritage Center in South-Central Los Angeles, where young people could come to play, learn, and be safe, instead of spending time on the streets. When she ran out of money, Myrtle sold her house rather than close the Center, for she appreciated the value of her endeavor. She truly believed that by giving to the community, she could make a difference.

In just five years, the Center became what Myrtle knew it could—a financially stable haven for young people. Appreciation of what can be done to help young people, rather than decrying how bad they are, allowed Myrtle to see the opportunity for a positive outcome within the tragic circumstance of her son's death.

Some crises are wider in scope. Societal crises affect communities or even entire nations. Appreciation can lift us out of the despair and sense of being overwhelmed that such crises bring. The September 11, 2001, terrorist attacks on the World Trade Center and the Pentagon occurred on a Tuesday. Our Appreciators Group met each Tuesday night. In shock, we didn't know what to do. Should we meet? Should we cancel? We decided to meet, and to see the day's horror as an opportunity to work with appreciation in a crisis. We reasoned that if appreciation wasn't helpful in the midst of tragedy, it wasn't worth much of anything.

Group members were somber, but all came. After every person shared their feelings about the day, we asked, "How can we use appreciation in this dreadful situation? What is there to appreciate in this crisis?"

There was, of course, the obvious: members appreciated their own, their friends', and their families' safety. They appreciated the courage and speed of the rescuers, and the miracles of survivors. The group found that appreciating the obvious soothed them and inspired them to hope on this dark day.

We wanted, however, to take appreciation further than using it to comfort ourselves. We wanted to use it proactively to attract something—we did not know what—that would counteract terrorism.

First, we discussed the definition of terrorism: the use of terror to achieve a political objective; to control and dominate by intimidation and violence. The essence of control or domination is to remove or limit someone's freedom. You control a dog by putting a leash on him, thereby restricting his freedom. We control prisoners by putting bars around them; we restrict their freedom. Terrorism fundamentally attacks freedom, first with violence, then with fear. The fear of future violence induces us to put bars around ourselves. We install metal detectors, hire security guards, and erect barricades. We travel less and are more wary of strangers. But when you remember that vibration entrains like vibration, you become reluctant to dwell on fear.

Rather than focus on and expand an energy of fear—"What other horrors are yet to come? We're not safe anywhere!"—which only increases terrorists' emotional and psychic hold on us, we decided that the way to counteract terrorism with appreciation would be to actively value and be grateful for freedom, not just our collective freedom as Americans, but the small daily freedoms we normally take for granted. The freedom to go anywhere or engage in just about any occupation, hobby, interest, or lifestyle. The freedom to disagree with your neighbor, the freedom to eat breakfast whenever you want—at midnight or 10:00 A.M.—the freedom to have a child, or five, or none, with or without a mate. The freedom to be a vegan or a meat-eater or anything in between. The freedom to say a morning prayer, or go jogging, or grab a coffee on your way to work. All of these precious personal freedoms make up so much of the goodness of our lives.

Since like attracts like, sending out a strong vibration of appreciation for the freedoms in our daily lives strengthens and expands the overall vibration of freedom in the world. Because you can't fear and appreciate simultaneously, the more you appreciate, the more you lessen the power of fear and the less you attract to be fearful of.

In the week that followed, it amazed us how often appreciation was on so many people's lips. People interviewed in the media repeated their heartfelt appreciation for the courage and perseverance of the rescue workers, the steadfastness of our country's leaders, the people who in the thick of horror called on cell phones to let others know what was happening and to give messages of love. Over and over, people talked about how they appreciated the kindness of strangers, the helping hands pitching in, the overwhelming response of Americans of every income level, ethnicity, age, and gender. We had never heard the word appreciation spoken so often.

On the following Tuesday, September 18, we had our next regularly scheduled Appreciators Group meeting. Members reported how appreciation had affected them, or how they had used it during the preceding week as they slowly emerged from shock and went about the business of recovery:

"I appreciate that I have a stable job; so many people are out of work, or going to be out of work because of this."

"I appreciate how unified we have become."

"I've been appreciating a man who was standing on the overpass at LAX, waving a huge American flag. Just standing there, waving and waving it. I appreciate that someone would do that, and no one would think he was crazy because we all knew what it meant."

"I realized as I worked with appreciating the freedom we enjoy in our day-to-day lives that I don't feel free. I have all these limitations and constraints on my personal freedom, and I realize I have to free myself of them."

"It's just miraculous and magical to see people appreciate each other, even people who usually wouldn't speak to each other."

"I was thinking of the plane crashes. I've been learning from them how important it is to keep my personal vibration strong so I'm prepared for whatever comes my way. I realize that appreciating brings me emotional strength."

"I realize my fear has been contributing to the overall field of terror. If I can pull away from that, and add light and goodness and appreciation, fear and hate can be dissipated. So I have been standing my own ground, knowing that I can create something better and more fulfilling."

Appreciation has a part to play in all crises, large and small, global or personal. There is so much in our everyday lives to cherish and hold close to our hearts when crisis hits. A poignant example came to us from the war in Iraq, which was just beginning as we were finishing this book. A Marine died in a helicopter crash. When his mother was interviewed on the news, she emphasized, in the midst of her grief, how important it is to remember that her son was doing exactly what he wanted to do and that he wouldn't have had it any other way. Appreciation of what is and what can be helps us heal and move on.

12

Towards a Future of   Appreciation

Appreciation matters. Appreciation matters to the lives we create in the here-and-now, but what of the future? What will it mean to our future if we appreciate now?

> We went through the whole positive-thinking era and that turned out to be lacking. Appreciation, if people really get the essence of it, is a different type of focus. It is active, for one thing. I think appreciation could heal wounds or wars, if used actively. I have seen it do so in my own life. Imagine if large groups of people committed to focusing appreciation for a common goal. The effect would be astounding.
>
> —Kim, Appreciators Group member

The key word, of course, is "active."

Ram Dass, in *Compassion in Action*, says that for love to be a healing agent, feelings of compassion must be acted upon rather than laying dormant in one's heart. So too with appreciation. When raised to the level of intention and action, appreciation may indeed "heal wounds or wars."

Why? Because those who value and are grateful for life and living do not seek to limit or control others. Those who appreciate life and living do not seek to destroy the world. Appreciators revel in life. They seek to make the world a better place for themselves and for others.

> I want us to use appreciation to make things better on a broader scale. If we all work on ourselves, learning to appreciate ourselves and others, maybe we can raise the universal consciousness.
>
> —Barbara, Appreciators Group member

Appreciation is essential to the survival and positive evolution of our world, for it is the capacity for appreciation that separates those who build the world from those who destroy it. Appreciation is as fundamental to world peace and prosperity as it is to individual happiness. It is the antithesis to a "tear-down" mentality, which sees destruction as a solution.

Since the events of September 11, 2001, awakened us abruptly to the preciousness of life, we as a nation have been rediscovering appreciation.

> Appreciation is a potent message and valuable tool for all of us, not in the old sense of "be grateful for what you have," but in the new awareness of how life is a wondrous opportunity. Appreciating ourselves and others, appreciating the things that we love about our life, appreciating freedom can only do us and the world a grand service. It seems it is where we are headed, and where global healing can begin.
>
> —Dan, Appreciators Group member

We can't go back to the old "I win, you lose" paradigm. We have learned that, globally, we are interconnected: what impacts one country's political or economic system ricochets into all others. "United we stand" is no longer applicable just to the United States. Instead, "united we stand" must be the new foundation for the survival of our planet and of the human race.

Appreciation … is a tulip bulb buried amongst the weeds, and if it is given any attention at all it will grow and multiply. Appreciation opens the way to positive futures that would not otherwise be available. This could have a dramatic impact on the world, politically and environmentally, making the planet safer for all its inhabitants.

—Teresa, Appreciators Group member

If our world is to survive, it will be because we learn to cooperate with each other to our mutual and respective advantages. Cooperation is best when based on appreciation, not fear. To enter a negotiation thinking, "I have to grab all I can, for fear that otherwise you will take some of what I need," is vibrational suicide. A whole different vibration is set up when we approach the negotiation table with appreciation: "I value and appreciate who you are and your right to argue for what you need, even as I value and appreciate who I am and my right to argue for what I need."

I approach conflict differently now. When I make myself stop and appreciate that this other person has what they believe is a legitimate point of view, I breathe easier. The urge to fight begins to dissolve.

—Sandy, Appreciators Group member

The more we learn to appreciate one another, despite our differences, the more likely we are to find world peace, and world peace is really the only way we can truly be at peace within our borders.

Where do we go from here? Appreciate ourselves, appreciate our lives. Allow the spillover of appreciation all around us to raise the vibration of the world, one human soul at a time—giving hope for mankind. A true and lasting way for the world to prosper.

I had a dream. That when we all just let go, and let appreciation fill our lives:

The floodgates will open,
the angels will sing,
the heralds will sound,
and love will reign upon the earth.

—Jan, Appreciators Group member

Indeed.

APPENDIX A

 The Appreciator's Code

1. *Appreciation is a vibration. Appreciation is a force. Appreciation is an energy.*

2. *You are a vibrational being. You emit frequencies of vibration.*

3. *Your vibration consists primarily of how you think and how you feel.*

4. *How you think and how you feel impact how you experience life.*

5. *You can choose what you think. Thinking changes how you feel.*

6. *Anything you focus on grows.*

7. *When you appreciate something or someone, you align yourself vibrationally with that thing or person.*

8. *When you align yourself with something, you draw more of it to you (like attracts like), and you expand your experience of that thing.*

9. *You can't align with something you're not. In other words, you can't be in a place of hate and align with love.*

10. *You don't have to wait for someone to appreciate you in order to appreciate them.*

APPENDIX B

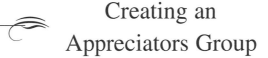

Creating an Appreciators Group

How can you find people who will support your exploration of the ways appreciation can benefit your life? Where do you find people to share their appreciation challenges, experiences, and tips with you?

There are "anonymous" support groups of almost every description—Alcoholics Anonymous, Codependents Anonymous, Overeaters Anonymous, Narcotics Anonymous, to name but a few. But nowhere could you find an "Appreciators Anonymous" or a "Gratitude Gathering."

Now you can. We have created a support group, which we call simply the "Appreciators Group, " where people can benefit from interaction with like-minded—or in this case, like-appreciating—individuals.

Anyone can start and conduct an Appreciators Group. All it takes is a few people wanting to meet regularly, usually once a week, to share their thoughts, feelings, and experiences of appreciation in a safe, supportive environment.

You also need a place to meet and a person willing to lead the group. You don't have to be a therapist or a health care professional to lead; anyone can do it. The leader is not there to analyze, diagnose, or provide treatment. This is not a therapy group, but a support group. And there needn't be just one leader; group members can take turns leading, if that better suits the group.

Once you have formed your group, you need to discuss whether you want it to be open or closed. A closed group starts out with a set group of members and is thereafter available only to those members; traditionally, however, support groups are open, meaning that new members may join at any time. Both open and closed groups work just fine. It is a good idea, however, in conducting an open group, to ask new members to read *The Power of Appreciation*, so that they have a clear idea of the group's focus. Support groups, whether open or closed, are generally not time-bound, meaning that the group tends to continue as long as the members want it to.

The Structure of an Appreciators Group Meeting

The structure of a meeting should include the following elements:

Information Giving

The group leader reads a passage or two from this book, to set the stage for that day's discussion. The group leader can choose to read passages from *The Power of Appreciation* sequentially (so that, over time, the entire book is read), or may choose to zero in on a topic of particular interest to the group at the time. For example, if a number of group members have chosen to improve or transform the relationship aspect of their lives, the group leader may choose to read selected and relevant passages from the relationship chapter. If group members appear to be more interested in the scientific aspect of appreciation, the group leader may decide that readings describing the vibrational nature of appreciation would be more appropriate for that week's meeting.

What drives the reading selection should always be what is of greatest concern to the group members. This does not mean that if the majority of the group is dealing with work issues, and that just one or two are dealing with crisis, that the group leader should only focus on work issues. The group leader must remain attentive to the needs and desires of the members and address them, even if sometimes that means saying, "We'll take a deeper look at crisis next week."

As part of information giving, the group leader should help the members define for themselves which aspect of their lives or which specific issue the members wish to improve, transform, or attract using appreciation. Each member should have at least one concern he or she is working on, and the group leader should keep track of each member's "appreciation-work-in-progress."

Sharing of Experiences

Sharing of experiences is probably the most important aspect of the meeting. The first sharing should revolve around the material read. The group leader invites discussion on the reading, especially in regard to resistances members have to appreciation in general, and to objections and difficulties they may anticipate in understanding or using appreciation as set forth in the reading. The leader encourages members to share whatever experiences they may have had that are relevant to the reading.

Sharing can then extend beyond the information given in the reading to a more general sharing of members' experiences with appreciation through the preceding week, as well as their progress (or lack thereof!) with whichever "appreciation-work-in-progress" each has chosen as his or her specific point of appreciative focus. Members should be encouraged to brainstorm together, to suggest different ways of applying appreciation, and generally to interact in learning more about the ins and outs of using appreciation.

The group leader functions primarily as a facilitator, and should not set himself or herself up as the "fixer" of problems, nor the keeper of appreciative wisdom. The group leader should help members stay on track, and speak to appreciation and its workings, rather than go on tangents about other ways of approaching their concerns. The leader should also be the timekeeper, and ensure that each person is given time to speak.

Suggestions for What to Be Working on Next

After sharing experiences, each member should commit to work on a specific aspect of appreciation during the following week. This may be a continuation of their current "appreciation-work-in-progress," or something new. If a member has trouble coming up with an idea, the leader or others should suggest possibilities. Decisions on what to work on, however, should always be left to the discretion of the individual member. This is a support group, not a class.

These are the basics. There are many other ways in which group leaders and members can enhance their experience of the group, such as keeping a group journal of successes members have had in using appreciation, or working on a group goal using appreciation. Readings from other authors that enhance and support appreciation can be used and discussed in addition to the information-giving readings. These and numerous other topics are addressed in the one-day training seminars we conduct to help people successfully create and run Appreciators Groups. Please contact us via our Web site, *www.thepowerofappreciation.net*, to learn more about our "How to Create and Run an Appreciators Group" seminar.

BIBLIOGRAPHY

Amen, Daniel G. *Healing the Hardware of the Soul*. Free Press, New York, 2002.

Beck, Aaron T. *Love Is Never Enough*. Harper & Row, New York, 1988.

Childre, Doc and Howard Martin. *The HeartMath Solution*. Harper, San Francisco, 1999, pp. 37, 40.

Chopra, Deepak. *Ageless Body, Timeless Mind*. Harmony Books, New York, 1993, p. 22.

Covey, Stephen R. *The Seven Habits of Highly Effective People*. Fireside, New York, 1989, p. 154.

Danner, D., D. Snowden, and W. Friesen. Positive emotions in early life and longevity: Findings from the nun study. *Journal of Personality and Social Psychology* 80(5): 804–13, 2001.

Dass, Ram. *Compassion in Action*. Bell Tower, New York, 1992.

Dossey, Larry. *Reinventing Medicine*. Harper, San Francisco, 1999, pp. 72–75.

Elium, Don and Jeanne Elium. *Raising a Son*. Beyond Words Publishing, Hillsboro, Oregon, 1992, p. 29.

Emmons, Robert A. The joy of thanks. *Spirituality & Health*, Winter 2002, Vol. 4, No. 4, 38–41.

Emoto, Masaru. *Messages from Water*. HADO Kyoikusha, Tokyo, 2000, pp. 74, 94, 96.

George, M. S. Brain activity during transient sadness and happiness in healthy women. *American Journal of Psychiatry*, March 1995, 1523: 341–51.

Goleman, Daniel. *Emotional Intelligence*, Bantam Books, New York, 1995, p. ix.

Gottman, John. *Why Marriages Succeed or Fail.* Fireside, New York, 1994, p. 72.

Hannaford, Peter. Aboard flight 564. *Washington Times*, Sept. 19, 2001.

HH Dalai Lama & Howard C. Cutler. Trans. Dr. Thupten Jinpa. *The Art of Happiness.* Riverhead Books, New York, 1998, p. 15.

Hillman, James. *The Force of Character.* Random House, New York, 1999, p. 17.

Hunt, Valerie. *Infinite Mind: The Science of Human Vibrations.* Malibu Publishing, Malibu, California 1989.

Kohn, Alfie. *No Contest.* Houghton Mifflin, New York, 1992, p. 7.

Langer, Ellen. *Mindfulness.* Perseus, New York, 1990.

Learning to walk again from experts in taking the first step. *Los Angeles Times*, March 10, 2002, Section A3.

Levine, Peter. *Waking the Tiger.* North Atlantic Books, Berkeley, California, 1997, p. 26–28.

Levy, Becca R., et al. Longevity increased by positive self-perceptions of aging. *Journal of Personality and Social Psychology* vol. 83, No. 2, August 2002.

Maman, Fabien. *The Role of Music in the Twenty-First Century.* Tama-Do Press, Redondo Beach, California, 1997.

McCullough, M., R. Emmons, & J. Tsang. The grateful disposition: a conceptual and empirical topography. *Journal of Personality and Social Psychology*, 82(1), 2002, 112–27.

Mehren, Elizabeth. University's leap of faith becomes lesson in community. *Los Angeles Times*, March 16, 2003.

Nelson, Noelle. *Winner Takes All: Exceptional People Teach Us How to Find Career and Personal Success in the 21st Century.* Perseus, New York, 1999, pp. 139, 210.

———. *Dangerous Relationships: How to Identify and Respond to the Seven Warning Signs of a Troubled Relationship.* Perseus, Cambridge, Mass., 2001.

Pert, Candace B. *Molecules of Emotion.* Simon & Schuster, New York, 1997, pp. 23, 135–37, 188–89, 285, 307.

Scaer, Robert C. *Trauma, Dissociation and Disease.* Binghamton, New York: Haworth Medical Press, 2001.

Schore, Allan N. *Affect Regulation and the Origin of the Self.* Lawrence Erlbaum Associates, New Jersey, 1994.

———. Effects of a secure attachment relationship on right brain development, affect regulation, and infant mental health. *Infant Mental Health Journal* 22(1–2), 2001, 7–66.

Seligman, Martin E. P. *Learned Optimism.* Pocket Books, New York, 1998, p.6.

Shafranske, Dr. Edward, 1988. Conversation with author.

Snider, Marie. "This side of 60 . . . Take charge of thriving longevity." *The Kansan Online,* www.thekansan.com.

Sternheimer, Joel. Physique theorique-musique des particules elementaires. (The music of the elementary particles.) *Comptes Rendus de L'Academie des Sciences: Mechanique-Physique Chimie Sciences de L'Univers et de la Terre,* 297 (Series 2), December 1983, 829–34.

Taylor, C. *The Physics of Musical Sounds.* American Elsevier Publishing, New York, 1965.

Tompkins, Peter. *The Secret Life of Plants.* Harper & Row, 1973, p. 18–19.

Uvnas-Mobert, K. Oxytocin linked antistress effects—The relaxation and growth response. *Acta Physiologica Scandinavica Supplement,* 640, 1997, 38–42.

Walter, Scott. "Personality." *Parade Magazine,* November 18, 2001.

To request your free biodot, send a self-addressed stamped envelope to *The Power of Appreciation*, 30765 Pacific Coast Highway, #132, Malibu, CA 90265, or go to *www.thepowerofappreciation.net*.

OTHER BOOKS FROM
BEYOND WORDS PUBLISHING, INC.

The Art of Thank You
Crafting Notes of Gratitude
Author: Connie Leas
$14.95, hardcover

While reminding us that a little gratitude can go a long way, this book distills the how-tos of thank-yous. Part inspirational, part how-to, *The Art of Thank You* will rekindle the gratitude in all of us and inspire readers to pick up a pen and take the time to show thanks. It stresses the healing power that comes from both giving and receiving thanks and provides practical, concrete, and inspirational examples of when to write a thank-you note and what that note should include. With its appealing and approachable style, beautiful gift presentation, charming examples, and real-life anecdotes, *The Art of Thank You* has the power to galvanize readers' resolve to start writing their all-important thank-you notes.

The Book of Intentions
Author: Dianne Martin
$16.95, hardcover

"*I intend.*" With those two words, our whole world can change. When we take notice of our intentions and take *control* of our intentions, we create a more harmonious and satisfying experience for ourselves and others. *The Book of Intentions* is a spiritual touchstone that will help you achieve your highest aspirations. In simple, resonant language, the book offers meaningful expressions of intention regarding all facets of existence, including family, friends, nature, society, and spirituality. Both powerful and practical, *The Book of Intentions* will help you take the first step in creating a more fulfilling life.

Forgiveness

The Greatest Healer of All

Author: Gerald G. Jampolsky, M.D.; Foreword: Neale Donald Walsch

$12.95, softcover

Forgiveness: The Greatest Healer of All is written in simple, down-to-earth language. It explains why so many of us find it difficult to forgive and why holding on to grievances is really a decision to suffer. The book describes what causes us to be unforgiving and how our minds work to justify this. It goes on to point out the toxic side effects of being unforgiving and the havoc it can play on our bodies and on our lives. But above all, it leads us to the vast benefits of forgiving.

The author shares powerful stories that open our hearts to the miracles which can take place when we truly believe that no one needs to be excluded from our love. Sprinkled throughout the book are Forgiveness Reminders that may be used as daily affirmations supporting a new life free of past grievances.

Seeing Your Life Through New Eyes

InSights to Freedom from Your Past

Authors: Paul Brenner, M.D., Ph.D., and Donna Martin, M.A.

$14.95, softcover

Seeing Your Life Through New Eyes is in a hands-on workbook format that helps you create a diary of self-discovery and assists you in resolving any misunderstood relationships. You can learn how to uncover unconscious patterns that define how you love, what you value, and what unique gifts you have in life. This book reveals those obstacles that too often interfere with loving relationships and creative expression, and it includes diagrams to use for your personal exploration and growth.

Your Authentic Self

Be Yourself at Work

Author: Ric Giardina

$14.95, softcover

Working people everywhere feel that they lead double lives: an "on the job" life and a personal life. Is it possible to live a life in which the separate parts of our personalities are united? In *Your Authentic Self*, author Ric Giardina explains that it is possible, and the key to achieving this integrated existence is authenticity. By honoring your authentic self at the workplace, you will not only be much happier, but you will also be rewarded with better on-the-job performance and more fulfilling work relationships. With straightforward techniques that produce instant results, this practical and easy-to-use guide will empower you to make the shift from seeing work as "off the path" of personal and spiritual growth to recognizing it as an integral part of your journey.

To order or to request a catalog, contact

Beyond Words Publishing, Inc.

20827 N.W. Cornell Road, Suite 500

Hillsboro, OR 97124-9808

503-531-8700

You can also visit our Web site at *www.beyondword.com* or e-mail us at *info@beyondword.com.*

Beyond Words Publishing, Inc.

OUR CORPORATE MISSION
Inspire to Integrity

OUR DECLARED VALUES
We give to all of life as life has given us.

We honor all relationships.

Trust and stewardship are integral to fulfilling dreams.

Collaboration is essential to create miracles.

Creativity and aesthetics nourish the soul.

Unlimited thinking is fundamental.

Living your passion is vital.

Joy and humor open our hearts to growth.

It is important to remind ourselves of love.